THE
JOB
SEARCH
TIME
MANAGER

Property of:

Name _____

Address _____

City, State, Zip _____

If found, please call collect (_____) _____

In case of emergency, call:

Name _____

Telephone _____

Ten Speed Press
Berkeley, California

TEN SPEED PRESS
P.O. Box 7123
Berkeley, CA 94707

Cover design by Fifth Street Design.
Text design by T. Craig Lincoln.

ISBN 0-89815-560-6
LC 93-25718

FIRST PRINTING 1993

Printed in the United States of America.

1 2 3 4 5 — 97 96 95 94 93

CONTENTS

I N S P I R A T I O N

Each person has his or her own vocation.

The talent is the call.

There is one direction in which all space is open to you.

You have faculties silently inviting you there

To endless exertion.

You are like a ship in a river;

You run against obstructions on every side but one;

On that side all obstruction is taken away,

And you sweep serenely over God's depths

Into an infinite sea.

— R A L P H   W A L D O   E M E R S O N

"SPIRITUAL LAWS"

If you're in the job market, you want a job quickly. Few job seekers—even high-level managers—can sustain a job search for more than three or four months without suffering. There's something inside us that says, "I have to be working . . . and I have to be working *now.*"

You need this book to organize you, to teach you the dos and don'ts of job hunting, to motivate, excite, and inspire you—and occasionally, to give you a good swift kick!

Job hunting is a tough road. The job search has been described as "the highest highs" and "the lowest lows." From beginning to end, it's an emotional roller coaster.

The market is highly competitive. There are usually more applicants than jobs, and supply exceeds demand. It's often lonely, because everyone else is working, and you have way too much free time.

In addition, job hunting is sales, and you're probably not a salesperson. More than likely, you're an accountant, a factory worker, a technical specialist, or a manager. Sales is unfamiliar, uncomfortable territory. Without help, you might make costly, time-consuming mistakes and stay unemployed longer than necessary. Why take a risk?

The eleven steps in career transition

Every job search is different. It's possible to talk to a recruiter or hiring manager, take a short interview, and be hired on the spot. But that's rare. It's more normal to agonize, to have ups and downs, to suffer rejection and disappointment, and to confront realities you don't like, either in yourself or in the world at large. Although every job hunt is different, a typical transition is somewhat predictable, and these are the eleven steps along the way:

1. *Job Loss.* Sometimes change is forced: you're fired outright or lose your job in a corporate reorganization. Other times, change is self-initiated: you lose faith in the boss, the company, your skills, or your career future—and *you* decide it's time to move on. Whether your change is forced or self-initiated, it's still difficult, because change itself is difficult.

2. *Focus.* You know you need a job, but you're not sure what to do. Should you continue on your current path or try something new? You're confused and need direction. You talk to friends, read career books, and seek advice. You want to choose the right course, and you're afraid to make a mistake.

3. *Resume.* Trying to get all your life experience onto one or two pages is frustrating, even angering. As you "waste time on the resume," you note a sense of urgency and begin to feel you're not getting anywhere.

4. *Letters.* You prepare letters to friends and begin answering want ads. Once your letters are in the mail, there's a lag time before the phone starts ringing. You're increasingly impatient.

5. *Networking/Meeting People.* Calling to ask for appointments is somewhat frightening. You feel like you're begging and "using your friends," but once you get the hang of it, it's great fun! You discover that others do want to help. However, you lose patience quickly, because informational meetings aren't "real interviews."

6. *Job Search.* You're now Vice President of Sales and Marketing for your own company, "Me, Inc." Hustle is the name of the game. You attend organizational meetings, write to companies, take friends to lunch, and do anything and everything possible to develop job leads.

7. *Interviewing.* The phone rings and you're invited to an actual job interview. You're scared and nervous. This could be the big one, and you could mess it up. You read books on interviewing, role-play difficult questions, and touch up your wardrobe. If the meeting goes well, you're high; if not, you're low. Either way, you're often kept waiting, and waiting is painful.

8. *Disappointment.* Midway in the process you "hit the wall." Although you've tried your best, you don't feel you've gotten anywhere. Nothing seems to be working. You get discouraged and feel you haven't done anything right. You get angry, irritable, and want to quit. Perhaps you can't get interviews; or if you can, no offer is forthcoming. Sometimes the perfect job you've been counting on falls through and you have to start over. Regardless of the reasons, you fight frustration, confusion, self-doubt, anger—and especially impatience.

9. *Job Offer.* Finally, you receive a specific job offer. It's not perfect, but it's worth discussing. This lifts your spirits. You get on the phone and fan the flames of other warm leads. If you're lucky, this produces a second or third offer.

10. *Salary Negotiations.* Most companies have fixed salary structures, and there isn't much room to negotiate. You negotiate within the limits. Usually, if you like the company and they like you, salary isn't a deal killer. You reach quick agreement.

11. *New Beginnings.* Once you accept an offer, you feel a tremendous sense of relief—and so do your family and friends. Now you can go back to being a human being. You feel good about life and look forward to your future. You send thank yous to everyone who's helped. "Next time," you say, "this whole process will be much, much easier. And I hope there is no 'next time.'"

PEANUTS

PEANUTS reprinted by permission of UFS, Inc.

How To Use The Job Search Time Manager

The Job Search Time Manager runs 90 days, because most well-organized campaigns are completed in that time. Besides a "To Do" list, each day includes a high-impact motivational quote, a word of advice from a hiring expert, and a world-class cartoon designed to put a smile in your day. We plan to pick you up and keep you moving!

The 90-day journal is divided into the eleven stages of a job campaign. Begin with the section that fits you; then move back and forth, as necessary. If your job campaign is unusual—say if you're *starting* with interviewing—simply turn to the appropriate section of the book.

Use the organizers on pages 188–204 to track your progress. Photocopy extra pages as you need them, but heed copyright laws and don't make copies for others.

This isn't a calendar; you'll need a desk or wall calendar to track the day and date. This is a job search project manager and companion. Carry it with you, and you'll always be organized. Doodle inside, mark it up, make notes in the margins. Fill it with want ads. Use it as a journal to record your feelings and progress.

Read and study the famous quotes, and take them to heart. These are the world's brightest voices. Let them sing inside your mind, and let them guide you. Always remember that today is important, that you are important, and that you have a very bright future.

Goethe said, "Nothing means more than this day." And he was right! Enjoy each day, even the difficult ones. As you move forward, have faith in yourself. Know that you're making progress even when you can't see it. Appreciate each moment for what it is. Understand that success is on the way. Sometime soon, you'll receive that special job offer; and when you do, I'd like to hear from you.

1
Job Loss

When one door of happiness closes, another opens; but often we look so long at the closed door that we do not see the one which has been opened for us.

—HELEN KELLER

Today's Day and Date
_____

To Do Checklist—Action Today
_____
_____
_____
_____

"A" Prospects
_____
_____
_____

Meetings/Appointments/Interviews

7:00 AM _____
_____

8:00 _____
_____

9:00 _____
_____

10:00 _____
_____

11:00 _____
_____

12:00 PM _____
_____

1:00 _____
_____

2:00 _____
_____

3:00 _____
_____

4:00 _____
_____

5:00 _____
_____

Evening _____

Job Search/Marketing Ideas
_____
_____
_____
_____
_____
_____
_____

To Mail or Ship
_____
_____
_____

Secretarial/Printing
_____
_____
_____
_____
_____

Pending
_____
_____
_____
_____

Today's 3 Accomplishments
_____
_____
_____
_____

EVERYONE SHOULD LOSE A JOB JUST ONCE. IT GIVES YOU A CLEARER PERSPECTIVE OF WORK AND HOW YOU FIT IN.

—HARVEY H. SIMS,
Director, Organization Development,
CoBANK

Notes

© ASHLEIGH BRILLIANT 1985.   POT-SHOTS NO 3848.

THE MOST IMPORTANT THING IN LIFE

IS TO BELIEVE THAT SOMETHING IN LIFE IS IMPORTANT.

Ashleigh Brilliant

Reprinted with permission.

9

2
Job Loss

ADVERSITY HAS THE EFFECT OF ELICITING TALENTS WHICH IN PROSPEROUS CIRCUMSTANCES WOULD HAVE LAIN DORMANT.

—HORACE

Today's Day and Date
_____

To Do Checklist—Action Today
_____
_____
_____
_____

"A" Prospects
_____
_____
_____

Meetings/Appointments/Interviews

7:00 AM _____
_____

8:00 _____

9:00 _____

10:00 _____

11:00 _____

12:00 PM _____

1:00 _____

2:00 _____

3:00 _____

4:00 _____

5:00 _____

Evening _____
_____

Job Search/Marketing Ideas
_____
_____
_____
_____
_____
_____
_____
_____
_____

To Mail or Ship
_____
_____

Secretarial/Printing
_____
_____
_____
_____
_____

Pending
_____
_____
_____
_____

Today's 3 Accomplishments
_____
_____
_____
_____
_____
_____
_____

When you're fired, look for the opportunity to learn, grow, and define yourself in a new context.

—DONALD F. SHAW,
Executive Vice President, ISEC

Notes

_____
_____
_____
_____
_____
_____
_____
_____
_____
_____
_____
_____
_____
_____
_____
_____
_____
_____

"I may not be much here in America . . . but in France, I'm a delicacy."

3
Job Loss

MAKE IT A RULE OF LIFE NEVER TO REGRET AND NEVER TO LOOK BACK. REGRET IS AN APPALLING WASTE OF ENERGY; YOU CAN'T BUILD ON IT; IT'S ONLY GOOD FOR WALLOWING IN.

—KATHERINE MANSFIELD

Today's Day and Date

To Do Checklist—Action Today

"A" Prospects

Meetings/Appointments/Interviews

7:00 AM

8:00

9:00

10:00

11:00

12:00 PM

1:00

2:00

3:00

4:00

5:00

Evening

Job Search/Marketing Ideas

To Mail or Ship

Secretarial/Printing

Pending

Today's 3 Accomplishments

12

*DON'T
BURN THE BRIDGE
TO YOUR LAST EMPLOYER;
YOU MAY NEED TO CROSS IT
FOR A REFERENCE.*

—ALAN M. FORKER
Career Consultant, **CareerLab**

Notes

KEEP A STIFF UPPER LIP

Copyright 1992 Bob Downs. Reprinted with permission.

Write injuries in sand, kindnesses in marble.

—FRENCH PROVERB

Today's Day and Date	Job Search/Marketing Ideas
To Do Checklist—Action Today	
"A" Prospects	
	To Mail or Ship
Meetings/Appointments/Interviews	
7:00 AM	
	Secretarial/Printing
8:00	
9:00	
10:00	
11:00	Pending
12:00 PM	
1:00	
2:00	
	Today's 3 Accomplishments
3:00	
4:00	
5:00	
Evening	

The best way to explain you've been laid off is to give a brief explanation of events that have faced the company and led up to your release—then move on.

—HARVEY H. SIMS,
Director, Organization Development,
CoBANK

Notes

© ASHLEIGH BRILLIANT 1985   POT-SHOTS NO. 3434.

Why is it that time softens some people, and hardens others?

Reprinted with permission.

OPPORTUNITY'S FAVORITE DISGUISE IS TROUBLE.

—FRANK TYGER

Today's Day and Date

To Do Checklist—Action Today

_____
_____
_____
_____

"A" Prospects

_____
_____
_____

Meetings/Appointments/Interviews

7:00 AM _____
_____
8:00 _____
_____
9:00 _____
_____
10:00 _____
_____
11:00 _____
_____
12:00 PM _____
_____
1:00 _____
_____
2:00 _____
_____
3:00 _____
_____
4:00 _____
_____
5:00 _____
_____
Evening _____
_____

Job Search/Marketing Ideas

_____
_____
_____
_____
_____
_____
_____
_____

To Mail or Ship

_____
_____
_____

Secretarial/Printing

_____
_____
_____
_____
_____
_____

Pending

_____
_____
_____
_____
_____
_____

Today's 3 Accomplishments

_____
_____
_____
_____
_____
_____

*If you're frustrated
and angry, talk to a counselor;
don't take it out on your family.
And also, don't kick your dog;
throwing your cat is OK.*

—ROBERT P. JUNK,
Executive Recruiter,
Phillips Personnel

Notes

SNAFU® by Bruce Beattie

SNAFU reprinted by permission of NEA, Inc.

*"The first part of the healing process is to get you to feel
good about how much I'm charging per hour."*

17

6
Job Loss

COMPASSION FOR ONESELF IS THE MOST POWERFUL HEALER OF THEM ALL.

—THEODORE ISAAC RUBIN

Today's Day and Date

_____

To Do Checklist—Action Today

_____
_____
_____
_____

"A" Prospects

_____
_____
_____

Meetings/Appointments/Interviews

7:00 AM _____
_____

8:00 _____

9:00 _____

10:00 _____

11:00 _____

12:00 PM _____

1:00 _____

2:00 _____

3:00 _____

4:00 _____

5:00 _____

Evening _____
_____

Job Search/Marketing Ideas

_____
_____
_____
_____
_____
_____
_____
_____

To Mail or Ship

_____
_____
_____

Secretarial/Printing

_____
_____
_____
_____
_____

Pending

_____
_____
_____
_____
_____

Today's 3 Accomplishments

_____
_____
_____
_____
_____
_____
_____

18

*It's important
to clear "old baggage"
as you go into the search—
develop a clean slate.*

—WILLIAM H. HECK,
Vice President Human Resources,
HCA Wesley Medical Center

Notes

POT-SHOTS NO. 2695.

Ashleigh
Brilliant

IT'S GOOD
TO KNOW
THAT,
EVEN IF
NOBODY
ELSE
NEEDS ME,
I STILL DO.

© ASHLEIGH BRILLIANT 1983.

Reprinted with permission.

19

7

Job Loss

No matter who or what made you what you have become, that doesn't release you from the responsibility of making yourself over into what you ought to be.

—ASHLEY MONTAGUE, PH.D.

Today's Day and Date

To Do Checklist—Action Today

_____
_____
_____
_____

"A" Prospects

_____
_____
_____

Meetings/Appointments/Interviews

7:00 AM _____

8:00 _____

9:00 _____

10:00 _____

11:00 _____

12:00 PM _____

1:00 _____

2:00 _____

3:00 _____

4:00 _____

5:00 _____

Evening _____

Job Search/Marketing Ideas

_____
_____
_____
_____
_____
_____
_____
_____

To Mail or Ship

_____
_____

Secretarial/Printing

_____
_____
_____
_____

Pending

_____
_____
_____
_____

Today's 3 Accomplishments

_____
_____
_____
_____
_____

20

DON'T TAKE TIME OFF. YOU CAN'T AFFORD A VACATION...YET.

—JAMES D. COLLINS,
VP Finance, XEL Communications

Notes

Berry's World

"Know what I hate—being rushed into adult roles before I'm ready."

8
Focus

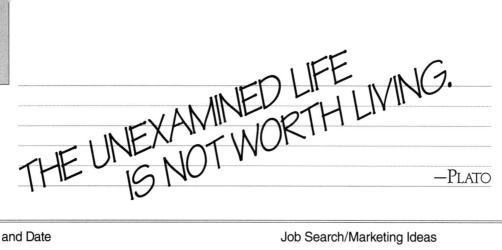

THE UNEXAMINED LIFE
IS NOT WORTH LIVING.

—PLATO

Today's Day and Date	**Job Search/Marketing Ideas**
To Do Checklist—Action Today	
"A" Prospects	**To Mail or Ship**
Meetings/Appointments/Interviews	
7:00 AM	**Secretarial/Printing**
8:00	
9:00	
10:00	
11:00	**Pending**
12:00 PM	
1:00	
2:00	**Today's 3 Accomplishments**
3:00	
4:00	
5:00	
Evening	

22

I see a lot of job hunters who aren't focused, and they will remain that way—job hunters.

—PAUL F. SHADDOCK,
Vice President Human Resources
United Technologies Microelectronics Center

Notes

ZIGGY®

YOUR APTITUDE TESTS INDICATE THAT YOU MIGHT MAKE A GOOD ECHO !!

2-11 Tom Wilson

9
Focus

CUT NOT THE WINGS OF YOUR DREAMS FOR THEY ARE THE HEARTBEAT AND THE FREEDOM OF YOUR SOUL.

—FLAVIA

Today's Day and Date

To Do Checklist—Action Today

_____
_____
_____
_____

"A" Prospects

_____
_____

Meetings/Appointments/Interviews

7:00 AM _____
_____
8:00 _____
_____
9:00 _____
_____
10:00 _____
_____
11:00 _____
_____
12:00 PM _____
_____
1:00 _____
_____
2:00 _____
_____
3:00 _____
_____
4:00 _____
_____
5:00 _____
_____
Evening _____
_____

Job Search/Marketing Ideas

_____
_____
_____
_____
_____
_____
_____

To Mail or Ship

_____
_____

Secretarial/Printing

_____
_____
_____
_____
_____

Pending

_____
_____
_____
_____
_____

Today's 3 Accomplishments

_____
_____
_____
_____
_____
_____

24

Three-fourths of career changers can't articulate the title/s of the job/s they are seeking.

—Betsy McGee,
Career Consultant, The McGee Group

Notes

PEANUTS reprinted by permission of UFS, Inc.

I THINK YOU'RE LETTING LIFE PASS YOU BY..

THERE MUST BE A THOUSAND THINGS YOU COULD BE DOING...

I AGREE, BUT BEING A DOG IS A FULL-TIME JOB..

10
Focus

> ## THE ONLY TRUE HAPPINESS COMES FROM SQUANDERING OURSELVES FOR A PURPOSE.
>
> —WILLIAM COWPER

Today's Day and Date
_____

To Do Checklist—Action Today
_____
_____
_____
_____

"A" Prospects
_____
_____
_____

Meetings/Appointments/Interviews

7:00 AM _____
_____

8:00 _____
_____

9:00 _____
_____

10:00 _____
_____

11:00 _____
_____

12:00 PM _____
_____

1:00 _____
_____

2:00 _____
_____

3:00 _____
_____

4:00 _____
_____

5:00 _____
_____

Evening _____
_____

Job Search/Marketing Ideas
_____
_____
_____
_____
_____
_____
_____

To Mail or Ship
_____
_____

Secretarial/Printing
_____
_____
_____
_____

Pending
_____
_____
_____
_____

Today's 3 Accomplishments
_____
_____
_____
_____
_____
_____

If you aren't focused, get prepared for a long, hard search.

—PAUL F. SHADDOCK,
Vice President Human Resources
United Technologies Microelectronics Center

Notes

ZIGGY copyright 1989 ZIGGY AND FRIENDS, INC. Dist. by UNIVERSAL PRESS SYNDICATE.
Reprinted with permission. All rights reserved.

No wind favors the person who has no destined port.

—MICHEL MONTAIGNE

Today's Day and Date

To Do Checklist—Action Today

_____
_____
_____
_____

"A" Prospects

_____
_____
_____

Meetings/Appointments/Interviews

7:00 AM _____

8:00 _____

9:00 _____

10:00 _____

11:00 _____

12:00 PM _____

1:00 _____

2:00 _____

3:00 _____

4:00 _____

5:00 _____

Evening _____

Job Search/Marketing Ideas

_____
_____
_____
_____
_____
_____
_____

To Mail or Ship

_____
_____

Secretarial/Printing

_____
_____
_____
_____
_____

Pending

_____
_____
_____
_____

Today's 3 Accomplishments

_____
_____
_____
_____
_____
_____
_____

MOST OF YOUR CONTACTS WANT TO HELP YOU GET A JOB, NOT IDENTIFY WHAT JOB YOU SHOULD BE SEEKING.

—BETSY MCGEE,
Career Consultant, The McGee Group

Notes

I WISH SOMETHING WOULD HAPPEN TO PUSH ME VIOLENTLY IN THE RIGHT DIRECTION.

Reprinted with permission.

29

12
Focus

DO NOT WISH TO BE ANYTHING BUT WHAT YOU ARE, AND TRY TO BE THAT PERFECTLY.

—St. Francis de Sales

Today's Day and Date

To Do Checklist—Action Today

_____
_____
_____
_____

"A" Prospects

_____
_____

Meetings/Appointments/Interviews

7:00 AM _____
_____
8:00 _____
_____
9:00 _____
_____
10:00 _____
_____
11:00 _____
_____
12:00 PM _____
_____
1:00 _____
_____
2:00 _____
_____
3:00 _____
_____
4:00 _____
_____
5:00 _____
_____
Evening _____

Job Search/Marketing Ideas

_____
_____
_____
_____
_____
_____

To Mail or Ship

_____
_____

Secretarial/Printing

_____
_____
_____
_____

Pending

_____
_____
_____
_____

Today's 3 Accomplishments

_____
_____
_____
_____
_____
_____

30

Unemployed job seekers are big believers in transferable skills. Hiring managers see no value in hiring transferable skills; they want specific related experience.

—ROBERT P. JUNK,
Executive Recruiter,
Phillips Personnel

Notes

STEIN

"Well, we have machines that shred paper. Do you have any other experience?"

13
Focus

The circumstances of your life have uniquely qualified you to make a contribution. And if you don't make that contribution, nobody else can make it.

—Rabbi Harold S. Kushner

Today's Day and Date

To Do Checklist—Action Today

_____

_____

_____

_____

"A" Prospects

_____

_____

Meetings/Appointments/Interviews

7:00 AM _____

8:00 _____

9:00 _____

10:00 _____

11:00 _____

12:00 PM _____

1:00 _____

2:00 _____

3:00 _____

4:00 _____

5:00 _____

Evening _____

Job Search/Marketing Ideas

_____

_____

_____

_____

_____

_____

_____

To Mail or Ship

_____

_____

_____

Secretarial/Printing

_____

_____

_____

_____

_____

Pending

_____

_____

_____

_____

_____

Today's 3 Accomplishments

_____

_____

_____

_____

_____

_____

*STAY FOCUSED.
THE SOONER YOU FINISH THIS JOB,
THE SOONER YOU CAN
START ONE THAT PAYS.*

—JAMES D. COLLINS
VP Finance, XEL Communications

Notes

Copyright 1993 Tom Cheney. Reprinted with permission.

"Dear Hiring Manager: In taking this long overdue opportunity to inform you of my change of address, I would like to inquire about my previous letter to you concerning your opening for a Marine Product Safety Officer."

14
Resume

SUCCESS IS NOT MEASURED BY WHAT YOU'VE DONE COMPARED TO OTHERS, BUT COMPARED TO WHAT YOU'RE CAPABLE OF DOING.

—ZIG ZIGLAR

Today's Day and Date

To Do Checklist—Action Today

_____

_____

_____

"A" Prospects

_____

_____

Meetings/Appointments/Interviews

7:00 AM _____

8:00 _____

9:00 _____

10:00 _____

11:00 _____

12:00 PM _____

1:00 _____

2:00 _____

3:00 _____

4:00 _____

5:00 _____

Evening _____

Job Search/Marketing Ideas

_____

_____

_____

_____

_____

_____

To Mail or Ship

_____

_____

Secretarial/Printing

_____

_____

_____

_____

Pending

_____

_____

_____

_____

Today's 3 Accomplishments

_____

_____

_____

_____

_____

_____

In the search process,
"puffing" is okay, even encouraged.
Lying is not.

—HARRY R. NEVLING,
SPHR, President, American Society
Healthcare Human Resources Association (ASHHRA)

Notes

Copyright 1993 Eli Stein. Reprinted with permission.

"I have to admit that what first attracted me to your
resume was this 'New and Improved' sticker on top."

35

15
Resume

We are what we repeatedly do. Excellence, then, is not an act but a habit.

—ARISTOTLE

Today's Day and Date

_____

To Do Checklist—Action Today

_____
_____
_____
_____

"A" Prospects

_____
_____

Meetings/Appointments/Interviews

7:00 AM _____
_____
8:00 _____
_____
9:00 _____
_____
10:00 _____
_____
11:00 _____
_____
12:00 PM _____
_____
1:00 _____
_____
2:00 _____
_____
3:00 _____
_____
4:00 _____
_____
5:00 _____
_____
Evening _____

Job Search/Marketing Ideas

_____
_____
_____
_____
_____
_____
_____

To Mail or Ship

_____
_____

Secretarial/Printing

_____
_____
_____
_____
_____

Pending

_____
_____
_____
_____
_____

Today's 3 Accomplishments

_____
_____
_____
_____
_____
_____
_____

Show me a person who can't distill a lifetime onto two pages and I'll show you a scatterbrain or an egomaniac.

—JIM KENNEDY,
Publisher, Directory of Executive Recruiters

Notes

Copyright 1993 Schwadron. Reprinted with permission.

"The mustard stains on your resume match those on your shirt. I like a man who's consistent."

YOU CAN'T BUILD A REPUTATION ON WHAT YOU ARE GOING TO DO.

—HENRY FORD

Today's Day and Date
_____

To Do Checklist—Action Today
_____
_____
_____
_____

"A" Prospects
_____
_____

Meetings/Appointments/Interviews

7:00 AM _____
_____

8:00 _____
_____

9:00 _____
_____

10:00 _____
_____

11:00 _____
_____

12:00 PM _____
_____

1:00 _____
_____

2:00 _____
_____

3:00 _____
_____

4:00 _____
_____

5:00 _____
_____

Evening _____
_____

Job Search/Marketing Ideas
_____
_____
_____
_____
_____
_____
_____

To Mail or Ship
_____
_____
_____

Secretarial/Printing
_____
_____
_____
_____
_____

Pending
_____
_____
_____
_____
_____

Today's 3 Accomplishments
_____
_____
_____
_____
_____
_____
_____
_____

Headhunters and hiring managers separate "wanna-be's" and "pretenders" from top candidates by selecting solid accomplishment records.

—KENNETH J. COLE,
Author, *The Headhunter Strategy*

Notes

"This isn't going to look very good on your resume."

GENIUS IS AN INFINITE CAPACITY FOR TAKING PAINS.

—JANICE ELICE HOPKINS

Today's Day and Date
_____

To Do Checklist—Action Today
_____
_____
_____
_____

"A" Prospects
_____
_____
_____

Meetings/Appointments/Interviews

7:00 AM _____
_____

8:00 _____
_____

9:00 _____
_____

10:00 _____
_____

11:00 _____
_____

12:00 PM _____
_____

1:00 _____
_____

2:00 _____
_____

3:00 _____
_____

4:00 _____
_____

5:00 _____
_____

Evening _____
_____

Job Search/Marketing Ideas
_____
_____
_____
_____
_____
_____
_____

To Mail or Ship
_____
_____
_____

Secretarial/Printing
_____
_____
_____
_____

Pending
_____
_____
_____
_____

Today's 3 Accomplishments
_____
_____
_____
_____

When I review a strong candidate's resume and find typographical errors, it's like running through an airport and hitting a stuck turnstile.

—WILLIAM A. RECTOR,
President, MicroLithics

Notes

"It says here in your resume that you're an experienced poofreader."

18
Resume

Virtually nothing comes out right the first time. Failures, repeated failures, are finger posts on the road to achievement. The only time you don't fail is the last time you try something, and it works. One fails forward toward success.

—CHARLES F. KETTERING

Today's Day and Date	Job Search/Marketing Ideas
To Do Checklist—Action Today	
"A" Prospects	To Mail or Ship
Meetings/Appointments/Interviews	
7:00 AM	Secretarial/Printing
8:00	
9:00	
10:00	
11:00	Pending
12:00 PM	
1:00	
2:00	Today's 3 Accomplishments
3:00	
4:00	
5:00	
Evening	

I expect candidates to analyze their failures and mistakes as well as their successes.

—LES A. WOLLER,
Director, Human Resources Planning & Development,
Battelle

Notes

Les Moore by Phillip Jewell

Copyright 1993 Phillip Jewell. Reprinted with permission.

NOT FAILURE, BUT LOW AIM, IS A CRIME.

—ERNEST HOLMES

Today's Day and Date	Job Search/Marketing Ideas
To Do Checklist—Action Today	
"A" Prospects	
	To Mail or Ship
Meetings/Appointments/Interviews	
7:00 AM	
	Secretarial/Printing
8:00	
9:00	
10:00	
11:00	Pending
12:00 PM	
1:00	
2:00	
	Today's 3 Accomplishments
3:00	
4:00	
5:00	
Evening	

Don't try gimmicks to get me to read your resume. It will surely find itself in the trash.

—RICHARD S. MACK,
Director of Personnel,
U.S. Olympic Committee

Notes

ZIGGY®

COPY SHOP

YOUR
RESUME
ON A
T-SHIRT
$17.95

2-11

20
Resume

In times of rapid change, experience is our worst enemy.

—J. Paul Getty

Today's Day and Date	Job Search/Marketing Ideas
To Do Checklist—Action Today	
"A" Prospects	To Mail or Ship
Meetings/Appointments/Interviews	
7:00 AM	Secretarial/Printing
8:00	
9:00	
10:00	
11:00	Pending
12:00 PM	
1:00	
2:00	Today's 3 Accomplishments
3:00	
4:00	
5:00	
Evening	

REMOVE ANY STATEMENT THAT MIGHT PROMPT THE READER TO ASK, "SO WHAT?"

—BETSY MCGEE,
Career Consultant, The McGee Group

Notes

Copyright 1993 H.L. Schwadron. Reprinted with permission.

"I'm quite impressed with your resume, except for this part about ten hours of T.V. every day since age six."

21
Letters

I'd rather attempt to do something great and fail than to attempt to do nothing and succeed.

—ROBERT SCHULLER

Today's Day and Date

To Do Checklist—Action Today

"A" Prospects

Meetings/Appointments/Interviews

7:00 AM

8:00

9:00

10:00

11:00

12:00 PM

1:00

2:00

3:00

4:00

5:00

Evening

Job Search/Marketing Ideas

To Mail or Ship

Secretarial/Printing

Pending

Today's 3 Accomplishments

A COVER LETTER
IS A 15-SECOND OPPORTUNITY
TO PROVE THAT YOU'VE
RESEARCHED THE COMPANY
MORE THOROUGHLY THAN
THE OTHER 500 CANDIDATES.

—WILLIAM A. RECTOR
President, MicroLithics

Notes

Copyright 1993 Tom Cheney. Reprinted with permission.

"No, no, no, Dan ... you don't indent your paragraphs in a block format, you're still going crazy with those commas, and now you're being redundant about your career goals ... please, I'm begging you ... go up in the attic and get your thesaurus."

IF YOU WANT TO SUCCEED
YOU SHOULD STRIKE OUT ON NEW PATHS
RATHER THAN TRAVEL THE WORN PATHS
OF ACCEPTED SUCCESS.

—JOHN D. ROCKEFELLER

Today's Day and Date

Job Search/Marketing Ideas

To Do Checklist—Action Today

"A" Prospects

To Mail or Ship

Meetings/Appointments/Interviews

7:00 AM

Secretarial/Printing

8:00

9:00

10:00

11:00

Pending

12:00 PM

1:00

2:00

Today's 3 Accomplishments

3:00

4:00

5:00

Evening

Job hunters who have a standard cover letter that doesn't apply to the job they are responding to make me feel they're not taking their job search seriously.

—CHERYL LEVITT,
Human Resource Specialist,
Robert Waxman, Inc.

Notes

"Wait a second! This is the same letter I found taped to my car windshield last week!"

23
Letters

IMAGINATION IS THE HIGHEST KITE THAT ONE CAN FLY.

—LAUREN BACALL

Today's Day and Date

_____

To Do Checklist—Action Today

_____
_____
_____
_____

"A" Prospects

_____
_____
_____

Meetings/Appointments/Interviews

7:00 AM _____
_____

8:00 _____
_____

9:00 _____
_____

10:00 _____
_____

11:00 _____
_____

12:00 PM _____
_____

1:00 _____
_____

2:00 _____
_____

3:00 _____
_____

4:00 _____
_____

5:00 _____
_____

Evening _____
_____

Job Search/Marketing Ideas

_____
_____
_____
_____
_____
_____
_____

To Mail or Ship

_____
_____
_____

Secretarial/Printing

_____
_____
_____
_____

Pending

_____
_____
_____
_____

Today's 3 Accomplishments

_____
_____
_____
_____
_____

Most of the letters
we receive are of such a
general nature they could
be applying for food stamps.

—LEO E. PERINO,
Director HR & FM,
Western Farm Bureau Life Insurance

Notes

© ASHLEIGH BRILLIANT 1983.

POT-SHOTS NO. 3063.
Ashleigh
Brilliant

YOU CAN'T REALLY
SPEED LIFE UP
OR
SLOW IT DOWN,

BUT
YOU CAN
CHANGE
ITS SHAPE
AND COLOR.

Reprinted with permission.

53

24
Letters

You can get what you want instead of having to want what you have. Success is easy after you believe. But first, you must believe.

—ZIG ZIGLAR

Today's Day and Date	Job Search/Marketing Ideas

To Do Checklist—Action Today

"A" Prospects

To Mail or Ship

Meetings/Appointments/Interviews

7:00 AM

Secretarial/Printing

8:00

9:00

10:00

11:00   **Pending**

12:00 PM

1:00

2:00

    Today's 3 Accomplishments

3:00

4:00

5:00

Evening

WHEN RESPONDING TO AN AD, MENTION POSITION— WE PLACE DOZENS OF ADS. WE DON'T WANT TO GUESS.

—BETTY HATCHER,
Human Resources Representative,
Penrose Hospital

Notes

Copyright 1993 Eli Stein. Reprinted with permission.

"The secret of success? Work diligently, be persistent, and never, never answer an employment ad that has a blind box number."

The most practical, beautiful, workable philosophy in the world won't work—if you won't.

—ZIG ZIGLAR

Today's Day and Date

To Do Checklist—Action Today

"A" Prospects

Meetings/Appointments/Interviews

7:00 AM

8:00

9:00

10:00

11:00

12:00 PM

1:00

2:00

3:00

4:00

5:00

Evening

Job Search/Marketing Ideas

To Mail or Ship

Secretarial/Printing

Pending

Today's 3 Accomplishments

ONLY 2 OF 10
WRITE THANK YOU NOTES
AFTER A JOB INTERVIEW OR
NETWORKING DISCUSSION.
DO YOU?

—ALAN M. FORKER,
Career Consultant, **CareerLab**

Notes

Les Moore by Phillip Jewell

ALL REAL LIVING IS MEETING.

—MARTIN BUBER

Today's Day and Date
_____

To Do Checklist—Action Today
_____
_____
_____
_____

"A" Prospects
_____
_____
_____

Meetings/Appointments/Interviews

7:00 AM _____
_____

8:00 _____
_____

9:00 _____
_____

10:00 _____
_____

11:00 _____
_____

12:00 PM _____
_____

1:00 _____
_____

2:00 _____
_____

3:00 _____
_____

4:00 _____
_____

5:00 _____
_____

Evening _____
_____

Job Search/Marketing Ideas
_____
_____
_____
_____
_____
_____
_____

To Mail or Ship
_____
_____

Secretarial/Printing
_____
_____
_____
_____

Pending
_____
_____
_____
_____

Today's 3 Accomplishments
_____
_____
_____
_____
_____
_____

Networking is the best search.

—HARRY R. NEVLING,
SPHR, President, American Society
Healthcare Human Resources Association (ASHHRA)

Notes

Les Moore by Phillip Jewell

Copyright 1993 Phillip Jewell. Reprinted with permission.

"Sometimes I think it would be easier just to do a little networking."

27
Networking

YOU DON'T HAVE TO BE GOOD TO START, BUT YOU DO HAVE TO START TO BE GOOD.

—TOM MALCOLM

Today's Day and Date

To Do Checklist—Action Today

_____
_____
_____
_____

"A" Prospects

_____
_____

Meetings/Appointments/Interviews

7:00 AM _____

8:00 _____

9:00 _____

10:00 _____

11:00 _____

12:00 PM _____

1:00 _____

2:00 _____

3:00 _____

4:00 _____

5:00 _____

Evening _____
_____

Job Search/Marketing Ideas

_____
_____
_____
_____
_____
_____
_____

To Mail or Ship

_____
_____

Secretarial/Printing

_____
_____
_____
_____

Pending

_____
_____
_____
_____

Today's 3 Accomplishments

_____
_____
_____
_____
_____
_____

60

When looking for a job, networking should occupy 60-70% of your time.

—ROY J. WILSON,
Senior VP, Human Resources,
Pearle Vision

Notes

Even people who are good at making other things often find it hard to make a start.

©ASHLEIGH BRILLIANT 1992 SANTA BARBARA
POT-SHOTS NO. 5736
Ashleigh Brilliant

Reprinted with permission.

28
Networking

Most people wait until everything is just right before they do anything. They refuse to go out on a limb because they don't understand that the fruit is always out on the limb.

—ZIG ZIGLAR

Today's Day and Date	Job Search/Marketing Ideas

To Do Checklist—Action Today

"A" Prospects

To Mail or Ship

Meetings/Appointments/Interviews

7:00 AM _____

Secretarial/Printing

8:00 _____

9:00 _____

10:00 _____

11:00 _____

Pending

12:00 PM _____

1:00 _____

2:00 _____

Today's 3 Accomplishments

3:00 _____

4:00 _____

5:00 _____

Evening _____

FIND A MENTOR—
SOMEONE WHO HAS A JOB
YOU'D LIKE SOMEDAY.
THEN ASK QUESTIONS.

—KAY TUBBS,
V.P. Regional Marketing,
NationsBank

Notes

ORGANIZATIONAL STRUCTURE

ME

EVERYBODY ELSE

BERNHARDT

Copyright 1993 Glenn Bernhardt. Reprinted with permission.

"Any questions?"

*People
may forget what you say,
but they will never forget
the way you made them feel.*

—Judy Sabah

Today's Day and Date	Job Search/Marketing Ideas

To Do Checklist—Action Today

"A" Prospects

To Mail or Ship

Meetings/Appointments/Interviews

7:00 AM

Secretarial/Printing

8:00

9:00

10:00

11:00

Pending

12:00 PM

1:00

2:00

Today's 3 Accomplishments

3:00

4:00

5:00

Evening

*A letter to friends
explaining your situation,
describing your ideal job,
and asking for advice and ideas
could be the most important letter
you will ever write.*

—WILLIAM S. FRANK,
Author, *200 Letters for Job Hunters*

Notes

ZIGGY

REASSURING
HUGS 25¢

3-18

GET HAPPINESS OUT OF YOUR WORK OR YOU MAY NEVER KNOW WHAT HAPPINESS IS.

—ELBERT HUBBARD

Today's Day and Date	Job Search/Marketing Ideas
To Do Checklist—Action Today	
"A" Prospects	
	To Mail or Ship
Meetings/Appointments/Interviews	
7:00 AM	
	Secretarial/Printing
8:00	
9:00	
10:00	
11:00	Pending
12:00 PM	
1:00	
2:00	
	Today's 3 Accomplishments
3:00	
4:00	
5:00	
Evening	

66

"Do you remember me?"
networking is usually
a waste of everyone's time.

—WILLIAM A. RECTOR
President, MicroLithics

Notes

Les Moore by Phillip Jewell

UNHAPPY
HOUR
5-6 PM

BAR

Copyright 1993 Phillip Jewell. Reprinted with permission.

*Enthusiasm
is the mother of effort,
and without it nothing great
was ever achieved.*
—RALPH WALDO EMERSON

Today's Day and Date

To Do Checklist—Action Today

"A" Prospects

Meetings/Appointments/Interviews

7:00 AM

8:00

9:00

10:00

11:00

12:00 PM

1:00

2:00

3:00

4:00

5:00

Evening

Job Search/Marketing Ideas

To Mail or Ship

Secretarial/Printing

Pending

Today's 3 Accomplishments

ENTHUSIASM IS A SALEABLE COMMODITY.

—ROBERT E. LUNDY,
Vice President of Administration,
Bellco Credit Union

Notes

LOUTHAN
© 1981 JOHN LOUTHAN

"Wake up, Mr. Densmore . . . the interview's over."

FORTUNE SIDES WITH THE PERSON WHO DARES.

—Virgil

Today's Day and Date

_____

To Do Checklist—Action Today

_____
_____
_____
_____

"A" Prospects

_____
_____

Meetings/Appointments/Interviews

7:00 AM _____
_____

8:00 _____

9:00 _____

10:00 _____

11:00 _____

12:00 PM _____

1:00 _____

2:00 _____

3:00 _____

4:00 _____

5:00 _____

Evening _____

Job Search/Marketing Ideas

_____
_____
_____
_____
_____
_____
_____

To Mail or Ship

_____
_____

Secretarial/Printing

_____
_____
_____
_____

Pending

_____
_____
_____
_____

Today's 3 Accomplishments

_____
_____
_____
_____
_____
_____

You have mastered the art of networking when you are offered referrals without asking for them.

—BETSY McGEE,
Career Consultant, The McGee Group

Notes

"I'm sorry, but Mr. Cremworth is too important to see you right now."

MY CREED IS THAT:
HAPPINESS IS THE ONLY GOOD.
THE PLACE TO BE HAPPY IS HERE.
THE TIME TO BE HAPPY IS NOW.
THE WAY TO BE HAPPY
IS TO MAKE OTHERS SO.

—ROBERT G. INGERSOLL

Today's Day and Date

To Do Checklist—Action Today

_____
_____
_____
_____

"A" Prospects

_____
_____

Meetings/Appointments/Interviews

7:00 AM _____

8:00 _____

9:00 _____

10:00 _____

11:00 _____

12:00 PM _____

1:00 _____

2:00 _____

3:00 _____

4:00 _____

5:00 _____

Evening _____

Job Search/Marketing Ideas

_____
_____
_____
_____
_____
_____

To Mail or Ship

_____
_____

Secretarial/Printing

_____
_____
_____
_____

Pending

_____
_____
_____
_____

Today's 3 Accomplishments

_____
_____
_____
_____
_____

Give as much as you get.
Start repaying unasked-for favors
by those who have helped
in your job search.

—BETSY MCGEE,
Career Consultant, The McGee Group

Notes

Copyright 1993 Barsotti. Reprinted with permission.

"Yes, most strangers are nice, but we bark at them all anyway."

73

Courage is doing what you're afraid to do. There can be no courage unless you're scared.

—EDDIE RICKENBACKER

Today's Day and Date

To Do Checklist—Action Today

"A" Prospects

Meetings/Appointments/Interviews

7:00 AM

8:00

9:00

10:00

11:00

12:00 PM

1:00

2:00

3:00

4:00

5:00

Evening

Job Search/Marketing Ideas

To Mail or Ship

Secretarial/Printing

Pending

Today's 3 Accomplishments

THE WORST MISTAKE IN NETWORKING IS ASKING FOR A JOB.

—LINDA K. BOUGIE,
Career Consultant, **CareerLab**

Notes

Copyright 1993 Eli Stein. Reprinted with permission.

35
Job Search

Whatever the mind of man can conceive and believe it can achieve.

—NAPOLEON HILL

Today's Day and Date	Job Search/Marketing Ideas
To Do Checklist—Action Today	
"A" Prospects	
	To Mail or Ship
Meetings/Appointments/Interviews	
7:00 AM	
	Secretarial/Printing
8:00	
9:00	
10:00	
11:00	Pending
12:00 PM	
1:00	
2:00	
	Today's 3 Accomplishments
3:00	
4:00	
5:00	
Evening	

STARTING A JOB SEARCH:
KEEP IN MIND THAT EVERYONE
GETS RE-EMPLOYED.
JUST STAY FOCUSED.

—PAUL F. SHADDOCK,
Vice President Human Resources,
United Technologies Microelectronics Center

Notes

Reprinted by permission: Tribune Media Services.

"Dear Lord, connect me with a firm of aggressive professionals with proven track records that will let me pursue rapid career growth with a team of professionals involved in state-of-the-art projects in a solid growth company."

CHANCE IS ALWAYS POWERFUL.
LET YOUR HOOK ALWAYS BE CAST.
IN THE POOL WHERE YOU LEAST
EXPECT IT, THERE WILL BE A FISH.

—OVID

Today's Day and Date

To Do Checklist—Action Today

_____
_____
_____
_____

"A" Prospects

_____
_____

Meetings/Appointments/Interviews

7:00 AM _____
_____
8:00 _____
_____
9:00 _____
_____
10:00 _____
_____
11:00 _____
_____
12:00 PM _____
_____
1:00 _____
_____
2:00 _____
_____
3:00 _____
_____
4:00 _____
_____
5:00 _____
_____
Evening _____
_____

Job Search/Marketing Ideas

_____
_____
_____
_____
_____
_____
_____

To Mail or Ship

_____
_____

Secretarial/Printing

_____
_____
_____
_____
_____

Pending

_____
_____
_____
_____

Today's 3 Accomplishments

_____
_____
_____
_____
_____
_____

I just surveyed my last 1500 customers to determine <u>how</u> executives, managers and professionals are finding jobs. Results: Networking, 40%; headhunters, 26%; direct approaches to employers, 17%; help wanted ads, 17%.

—KENNETH J. COLE,
Publisher, *The Recruiting & Search Report*

Notes

37
Job Search

*I don't like work—
no one does—but what I like
is in the work—the chance
to find yourself.*

—JOSEPH CONRAD

Today's Day and Date	Job Search/Marketing Ideas

To Do Checklist—Action Today

"A" Prospects

To Mail or Ship

Meetings/Appointments/Interviews

7:00 AM

8:00

9:00

Secretarial/Printing

10:00

11:00

Pending

12:00 PM

1:00

2:00

Today's 3 Accomplishments

3:00

4:00

5:00

Evening

CONSIDER
YOUR SEARCH TO BE
THE TOUGHEST JOB
YOU'LL EVER HAVE.

—DAVID A. SWAN,
VP Human Resources,
Leprino Foods

Notes

THE EASY WAY
THROUGH
LIFE

IS NOT
NECESSARILY
THE
MOST
ENJOYABLE
ONE.

© ASHLEIGH BRILLIANT 1987.

POT-SHOTS
NO. 4099.

Reprinted with permission.

81

*Everything comes
to the person who hustles
while they wait.*

—THOMAS EDISON

Today's Day and Date

_____

To Do Checklist—Action Today

_____
_____
_____
_____

"A" Prospects

_____
_____
_____

Meetings/Appointments/Interviews

7:00 AM _____
_____
8:00 _____
_____
9:00 _____
_____
10:00 _____
_____
11:00 _____
_____
12:00 PM _____
_____
1:00 _____
_____
2:00 _____
_____
3:00 _____
_____
4:00 _____
_____
5:00 _____
_____
Evening _____
_____

Job Search/Marketing Ideas

_____
_____
_____
_____
_____
_____
_____

To Mail or Ship

_____
_____
_____

Secretarial/Printing

_____
_____
_____
_____
_____

Pending

_____
_____
_____
_____
_____

Today's 3 Accomplishments

_____
_____
_____
_____
_____
_____
_____

Activity level is the most important determinant of job hunting success. Finders out-hustle non-finders by double or triple the level of activity.

—KENNETH J. COLE,
Publisher, *The Recruiting & Search Report*

Notes

Copyright 1993 Tom Cheney. Reprinted with permission.

"We're a fast-paced and rapidly expanding corporation. Leave your resume with my secretary and I'll pick it up on the next lap!"

*I don't believe in circumstances.
The people who get on in this world
are the people who get up and look
for circumstances they want.*

—GEORGE BERNARD SHAW

Today's Day and Date

To Do Checklist—Action Today

_____
_____
_____
_____

"A" Prospects

_____
_____

Meetings/Appointments/Interviews

7:00 AM _____

8:00 _____

9:00 _____

10:00 _____

11:00 _____

12:00 PM _____

1:00 _____

2:00 _____

3:00 _____

4:00 _____

5:00 _____

Evening _____

Job Search/Marketing Ideas

_____
_____
_____
_____
_____
_____

To Mail or Ship

_____
_____

Secretarial/Printing

_____
_____
_____
_____

Pending

_____
_____
_____
_____

Today's 3 Accomplishments

_____
_____
_____
_____
_____

WHEN YOU'RE ENGAGED IN A JOB SEARCH YOU ARE RUNNING A "PLACEMENT BUSINESS"— RUN IT LIKE A BUSINESS.

—BERNARD M. CURTIS,
Regional Director of Training,
ITT Sheraton

Notes

$25,000--
AS IS.

40
Job Search

THE BASIC GOAL-REACHING PRINCIPLE: GO AS FAR AS YOU CAN SEE AND WHEN YOU GET THERE, YOU WILL BE ABLE TO SEE FARTHER.

—ZIG ZIGLAR

Today's Day and Date	Job Search/Marketing Ideas
To Do Checklist—Action Today	
"A" Prospects	To Mail or Ship
Meetings/Appointments/Interviews	
7:00 AM	Secretarial/Printing
8:00	
9:00	
10:00	
11:00	Pending
12:00 PM	
1:00	
2:00	Today's 3 Accomplishments
3:00	
4:00	
5:00	
Evening	

*Want a job?
Stay away from the
employment office ... find out
who makes the decisions
and how people are really hired.
Pursue those contacts first!*

—EDWARD P. BEHLKE,
Vice President Human Resources,
King Soopers

Notes

"Two N's and one L? Are you sure?"

Copyright 1993 Eli Stein. Reprinted with permission.

You're getting what you're getting because you're doing what you're doing.

—Dr. Robert Schuller

Today's Day and Date	Job Search/Marketing Ideas
To Do Checklist—Action Today	
"A" Prospects	To Mail or Ship
Meetings/Appointments/Interviews	
7:00 AM	Secretarial/Printing
8:00	
9:00	
10:00	
11:00	Pending
12:00 PM	
1:00	
2:00	Today's 3 Accomplishments
3:00	
4:00	
5:00	
Evening	

MOST JOB HUNTING BOOKS
ARE OUT OF DATE FOR TODAY'S
TIGHT MARKET AND NEW
WAY OF "GETTING AHEAD."
WHAT WORKED 10–15 YEARS AGO
DOESN'T WORK TODAY.

—KAY TUBBS,
VP Regional Marketing,
NationsBank

Notes

*"For the past ten years, there was a demand for movers and shakers.
Now all of a sudden, there seems to be a demand again for relaxers."*

89

42
Job Search

THERE IS NO POINT IN DOING WELL THAT WHICH YOU SHOULD NOT BE DOING AT ALL.

—THOMAS K. CONNELLAN

Today's Day and Date
_____

To Do Checklist—Action Today
_____
_____
_____
_____

"A" Prospects
_____
_____

Meetings/Appointments/Interviews

7:00 AM _____

8:00 _____

9:00 _____

10:00 _____

11:00 _____

12:00 PM _____

1:00 _____

2:00 _____

3:00 _____

4:00 _____

5:00 _____

Evening _____

Job Search/Marketing Ideas
_____
_____
_____
_____
_____
_____
_____
_____

To Mail or Ship
_____
_____

Secretarial/Printing
_____
_____
_____
_____
_____

Pending
_____
_____
_____
_____

Today's 3 Accomplishments
_____
_____
_____
_____
_____

90

Some companies may look for candidates who break the rules to get an interview. In our company, a rule-breaker would not get anywhere because we treat each candidate with the same degree of consideration. A squeaky wheel would just be . . . noisy.

—SHARON ALMIRALL,
Marketing Director,
Duluth News-Tribune

Notes

BERRY'S WORLD reprinted by permission of NEA, Inc.

"So, one day, I decided to get into a field where there aren't many women . . ."

43
Job Search

We don't live in a world of reality, we live in a world of perceptions.

—J. GERALD SIMMONS

Today's Day and Date
_____

To Do Checklist—Action Today
_____
_____
_____
_____

"A" Prospects
_____
_____

Meetings/Appointments/Interviews

7:00 AM _____
_____

8:00 _____
_____

9:00 _____
_____

10:00 _____
_____

11:00 _____
_____

12:00 PM _____
_____

1:00 _____
_____

2:00 _____
_____

3:00 _____
_____

4:00 _____
_____

5:00 _____
_____

Evening _____

Job Search/Marketing Ideas
_____
_____
_____
_____
_____
_____
_____

To Mail or Ship
_____
_____
_____

Secretarial/Printing
_____
_____
_____
_____
_____

Pending
_____
_____
_____
_____

Today's 3 Accomplishments
_____
_____
_____
_____
_____
_____

ANY PHONE NUMBERS
ON THE RESUME SHOULD
ACTUALLY BE ANSWERED—
IF ONLY BY A MACHINE.
I WON'T CALL TWICE.

—SHARON ALMIRALL,
Marketing Director,
Duluth News-Tribune

Notes

CHARLIE

...IF WHEN YOU HEAR THE TONE YOU HANG UP INSTEAD OF LEAVING A MESSAGE, YOUR NUMBER WILL BE TRACED DOWN AND YOU WILL BE GIVEN A THRASHING! SO, BE SMART. LEAVE A MESSAGE!

11-25

© 1981 by Chicago Tribune-N.Y. News Synd. Inc.
All Rights Reserved

Reprinted by permission: Tribune Media Services.

WHEN WE ARE NOT SURE, WE ARE ALIVE.

—GRAHAM GREENE

Today's Day and Date

_____

To Do Checklist—Action Today

_____
_____
_____
_____

"A" Prospects

_____
_____
_____

Meetings/Appointments/Interviews

7:00 AM _____
_____

8:00 _____
_____

9:00 _____
_____

10:00 _____
_____

11:00 _____
_____

12:00 PM _____
_____

1:00 _____
_____

2:00 _____
_____

3:00 _____
_____

4:00 _____
_____

5:00 _____
_____

Evening _____
_____

Job Search/Marketing Ideas

_____
_____
_____
_____
_____
_____

To Mail or Ship

_____
_____
_____

Secretarial/Printing

_____
_____
_____
_____
_____

Pending

_____
_____
_____
_____
_____

Today's 3 Accomplishments

_____
_____
_____
_____
_____
_____

94

There is a good chance that the person conducting your interview has lost a job or two and knows how it feels.

—HARVEY H. SIMS,
Director, Organization Development,
CoBANK

Notes

"I'm looking for a job myself."

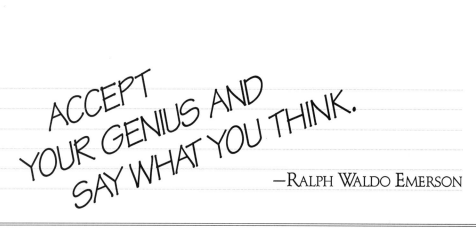

—Ralph Waldo Emerson

Today's Day and Date

_____

To Do Checklist—Action Today

_____
_____
_____
_____

"A" Prospects

_____
_____
_____

Meetings/Appointments/Interviews

7:00 AM _____
_____

8:00 _____
_____

9:00 _____
_____

10:00 _____
_____

11:00 _____
_____

12:00 PM _____
_____

1:00 _____
_____

2:00 _____
_____

3:00 _____
_____

4:00 _____
_____

5:00 _____
_____

Evening _____

Job Search/Marketing Ideas

_____
_____
_____
_____
_____
_____
_____

To Mail or Ship

_____
_____

Secretarial/Printing

_____
_____
_____
_____

Pending

_____
_____
_____
_____

Today's 3 Accomplishments

_____
_____
_____
_____
_____

Go to a couple of interviews right off the bat. Make a fool of yourself and get it over with. You'll be fine after that.

—KERRI S. SMITH,
Careers Reporter,
The Rocky Mountain News

Notes

Copyright 1993 Eli Stein. Reprinted with permission.

"Congratulations! You've lit up the entire board!"

EVERY ARTIST WAS FIRST AN AMATEUR.

—Ralph Waldo Emerson

Today's Day and Date

To Do Checklist—Action Today

"A" Prospects

Meetings/Appointments/Interviews

7:00 AM

8:00

9:00

10:00

11:00

12:00 PM

1:00

2:00

3:00

4:00

5:00

Evening

Job Search/Marketing Ideas

To Mail or Ship

Secretarial/Printing

Pending

Today's 3 Accomplishments

98

Interviewing is an art. You only get better by practice.

—BOB SCHULZ,
Director of Personnel,
Jones Intercable

Notes

Reprinted with permission: Tribune Media Services

99

A smooth sea never made a skilled mariner.

—ENGLISH PROVERB

Today's Day and Date	**Job Search/Marketing Ideas**
_____	_____

Today's Day and Date
_____

To Do Checklist—Action Today
_____
_____
_____
_____

"A" Prospects
_____
_____
_____

Meetings/Appointments/Interviews

7:00 AM _____
_____

8:00 _____
_____

9:00 _____
_____

10:00 _____
_____

11:00 _____
_____

12:00 PM _____
_____

1:00 _____
_____

2:00 _____
_____

3:00 _____
_____

4:00 _____
_____

5:00 _____
_____

Evening _____
_____

Job Search/Marketing Ideas
_____
_____
_____
_____
_____
_____
_____

To Mail or Ship
_____
_____

Secretarial/Printing
_____
_____
_____
_____
_____

Pending
_____
_____
_____
_____

Today's 3 Accomplishments
_____
_____
_____
_____
_____
_____
_____

Never pass up an interview, no matter how little promise it may appear to have.

—DAVID A. SWAN,
VP Human Resources,
Leprino Foods

Notes

Tense moments #47: The old roll top desk interview.

FEW WISHES COME TRUE BY THEMSELVES.

—June Smith

Today's Day and Date

To Do Checklist—Action Today

"A" Prospects

Meetings/Appointments/Interviews

7:00 AM

8:00

9:00

10:00

11:00

12:00 PM

1:00

2:00

3:00

4:00

5:00

Evening

Job Search/Marketing Ideas

To Mail or Ship

Secretarial/Printing

Pending

Today's 3 Accomplishments

Go to outrageous steps to learn anything you possibly can about the company and people.

—RICHARD J. MASEK,
Director,
Affiliated Personnel Advisors

Notes

Copyright 1993 Eli Stein. Reprinted with permission.

"We're either under-staffed or over-desked."

Far better it is to dare mighty things, even though checkered by failure, than to take rank with those who neither enjoy much or suffer much, because they live in the gray twilight that knows not victory nor defeat.

—THEODORE ROOSEVELT

Today's Day and Date

To Do Checklist—Action Today

"A" Prospects

Meetings/Appointments/Interviews

7:00 AM

8:00

9:00

10:00

11:00

12:00 PM

1:00

2:00

3:00

4:00

5:00

Evening

Job Search/Marketing Ideas

To Mail or Ship

Secretarial/Printing

Pending

Today's 3 Accomplishments

A GOOD JOB CANDIDATE WILL BE ABLE TO TELL ME THINGS ABOUT MY COMPANY I DIDN'T KNOW.

—BOB SCHULZ,
Director of Personnel,
Jones Intercable

Notes

HERMAN

"The man we're looking for will be dynamic and aggressive."

SELLING IS 98% UNDERSTANDING HUMAN BEINGS, AND 2% PRODUCT KNOWLEDGE.

—JOE GANDOLFO, CLU

Today's Day and Date

To Do Checklist—Action Today

"A" Prospects

Meetings/Appointments/Interviews

7:00 AM

8:00

9:00

10:00

11:00

12:00 PM

1:00

2:00

3:00

4:00

5:00

Evening

Job Search/Marketing Ideas

To Mail or Ship

Secretarial/Printing

Pending

Today's 3 Accomplishments

Likeability, chemistry, and technical knowledge are the three most important elements of a successful interview. In that order!

—BETSY MCGEE,
Career Consultant, The McGee Group

Notes

Copyright 1993 Eli Stein. Reprinted with permission.

"I'm sorry, but we're looking for someone just a little more dynamic, perceptive, articulate, incisive, flexible, astute, gregarious, prudent, forceful, motivated, clear-headed, versatile, magnetic, and self-propelled."

51
Interviewing

Successes like pleasing results...
failures like pleasing methods.

—CAVETT ROBERT

Today's Day and Date

To Do Checklist—Action Today

_____
_____
_____
_____

"A" Prospects

_____
_____

Meetings/Appointments/Interviews

7:00 AM _____
_____

8:00 _____

9:00 _____

10:00 _____

11:00 _____

12:00 PM _____

1:00 _____

2:00 _____

3:00 _____

4:00 _____

5:00 _____

Evening _____

Job Search/Marketing Ideas

_____
_____
_____
_____
_____
_____

To Mail or Ship

_____
_____

Secretarial/Printing

_____
_____
_____
_____

Pending

_____
_____
_____
_____

Today's 3 Accomplishments

_____
_____
_____

It's hard to believe that candidates would show up for a professional position dressed in playwear, but it happens all the time. They should come to the interview dressed as they would if they had the job.

—SHARON ALMIRALL,
Marketing Director,
Duluth News-Tribune

Notes

INTERVIEW GREMLINS

CONTACT LENS POPS OUT

STUBBORN COWLICK

NOSE BLEED

HICCUPS

PEN LEAKS

BUTTON FALLS OFF

BRIEF CASE LATCHES FAIL

CHANGE FALLS THROUGH HOLE IN POCKET

CHENEY

Copyright 1993 Tom Cheney. Reprinted with permission.

Take therefore no thought for the morrow: for the morrow shall take thought for the things of itself.

—MATTHEW 6:25

Today's Day and Date

To Do Checklist—Action Today

_____
_____
_____
_____

"A" Prospects

_____
_____

Meetings/Appointments/Interviews

7:00 AM _____

8:00 _____

9:00 _____

10:00 _____

11:00 _____

12:00 PM _____

1:00 _____

2:00 _____

3:00 _____

4:00 _____

5:00 _____

Evening _____

Job Search/Marketing Ideas

_____
_____
_____
_____
_____
_____
_____

To Mail or Ship

_____
_____

Secretarial/Printing

_____
_____
_____
_____

Pending

_____
_____
_____

Today's 3 Accomplishments

_____
_____
_____
_____
_____

*TALK CAREER, NOT JOB. LET
THE INTERVIEWER KNOW YOU ARE
A BIG-PICTURE PERSON.*

—SCOTT G. HOWARD,
President,
Reid Merrill Brunson & Associates

Notes

Copyright 1980 Artemus Cole. Reprinted with permission.

"What do you mean, you want SUNDAYS off?"

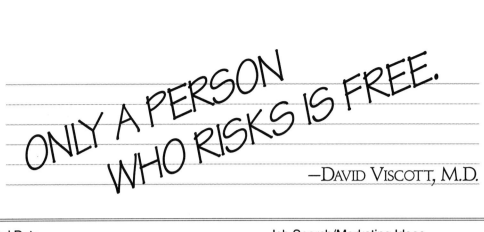

ONLY A PERSON WHO RISKS IS FREE.

—David Viscott, M.D.

Today's Day and Date

To Do Checklist—Action Today

_____
_____
_____

"A" Prospects

_____
_____

Meetings/Appointments/Interviews

7:00 AM _____

8:00 _____

9:00 _____

10:00 _____

11:00 _____

12:00 PM _____

1:00 _____

2:00 _____

3:00 _____

4:00 _____

5:00 _____

Evening _____

Job Search/Marketing Ideas

_____
_____
_____
_____
_____
_____
_____

To Mail or Ship

_____
_____

Secretarial/Printing

_____
_____
_____
_____

Pending

_____
_____
_____
_____

Today's 3 Accomplishments

_____
_____
_____
_____
_____
_____

112

I hate it when I feel interviewees are saying what they think I want to hear.

—BERNARD M. CURTIS,
Regional Director of Training,
ITT Sheraton

Notes

"Sure I'm exaggerating everything . . . aren't you?"

THE BEST WAY TO DISCOVER ONE'S IDENTITY IS TO SEEK A HIGH GOAL WITH ALL ONE'S ENERGY. SUCCESS FALLS MORE TO THE COURAGEOUS THAN TO THOSE WHO UNDERSTAND AND PLAN EVERYTHING BUT CAN'T ACT.

—DAVID VISCOTT, M.D.

Today's Day and Date

To Do Checklist—Action Today

"A" Prospects

Meetings/Appointments/Interviews

7:00 AM

8:00

9:00

10:00

11:00

12:00 PM

1:00

2:00

3:00

4:00

5:00

Evening

Job Search/Marketing Ideas

To Mail or Ship

Secretarial/Printing

Pending

Today's 3 Accomplishments

Know your three or four strengths and be able to summarize them within 30 seconds.

—BRUCE PERCH,
Director of Finance/Operations,
American Cancer Society

Notes

Copyright 1993 Eli Stein. Reprinted with permission.

"I want to make it perfectly clear that I'm not turning you down because you're a woman, or because of your age or marital status—I'm turning you down because, in my opinion, you're a chowderhead."

55
Interviewing

GREAT ACHIEVEMENT IS USUALLY BORN OF GREAT SACRIFICE, AND IS NEVER THE RESULT OF SELFISHNESS.

—NAPOLEON HILL

Today's Day and Date	Job Search/Marketing Ideas
To Do Checklist—Action Today	
"A" Prospects	To Mail or Ship
Meetings/Appointments/Interviews	
7:00 AM	Secretarial/Printing
8:00	
9:00	
10:00	
11:00	Pending
12:00 PM	
1:00	
2:00	Today's 3 Accomplishments
3:00	
4:00	
5:00	
Evening	

116

I don't hire people who are outwardly more concerned with their own needs than the company's needs.

—JENNIFER CRAIG,
Executive Vice President,
Reid Merrill Brunson & Associates

Notes

"Can we discuss salary first? My wife's waiting to go shopping."

117

56
Interviewing

If one advances confidently in the direction of his dreams, and endeavors to live the life that only he has imagined, he will meet with a success unexpected in common hours.

—HENRY DAVID THOREAU

Today's Day and Date

_____

To Do Checklist—Action Today

_____
_____
_____
_____

"A" Prospects

_____
_____

Meetings/Appointments/Interviews

7:00 AM _____
_____
8:00 _____
_____
9:00 _____
_____
10:00 _____
_____
11:00 _____
_____
12:00 PM _____
_____
1:00 _____
_____
2:00 _____
_____
3:00 _____
_____
4:00 _____
_____
5:00 _____
_____
Evening _____
_____

Job Search/Marketing Ideas

_____
_____
_____
_____
_____
_____

To Mail or Ship

_____
_____

Secretarial/Printing

_____
_____
_____
_____
_____

Pending

_____
_____
_____
_____
_____

Today's 3 Accomplishments

_____
_____
_____
_____
_____
_____
_____

DON'T ARRIVE TOO EARLY. INTERVIEWERS ARE BUSY, BUT ALSO COMPASSIONATE, AND THEY MAY FEEL UNEASY KEEPING YOU WAITING SO LONG.

—BETTY HATCHER,
Human Resources Representative,
Penrose Hospital

Notes

PORTERFIELD

Reprinted with special permission of North America Syndicate.

"If this bothers you, I can hire someone else."

You're a winner when you have a life you love.

—JERRY GILLIES

Today's Day and Date	Job Search/Marketing Ideas
To Do Checklist—Action Today	
"A" Prospects	
	To Mail or Ship
Meetings/Appointments/Interviews	
7:00 AM	Secretarial/Printing
8:00	
9:00	
10:00	
11:00	Pending
12:00 PM	
1:00	
2:00	Today's 3 Accomplishments
3:00	
4:00	
5:00	
Evening	

Be prepared to answer abstract questions that reveal your personality, e.g., "Describe the funniest moment of your life!"

—EDWARD P. BEHLKE,
Vice President Human Resources,
King Soopers

Notes

"If we were to hire you, would you be willing to answer more absurd hypothetical questions like this one?"

58
Interviewing

ONE DOESN'T DISCOVER NEW LANDS WITHOUT CONSENTING TO LOSE SIGHT OF THE SHORE FOR A VERY LONG TIME.

—ANDRÉ GIDE

Today's Day and Date

To Do Checklist—Action Today

_____
_____
_____
_____

"A" Prospects

_____
_____

Meetings/Appointments/Interviews

7:00 AM _____

8:00 _____

9:00 _____

10:00 _____

11:00 _____

12:00 PM _____

1:00 _____

2:00 _____

3:00 _____

4:00 _____

5:00 _____

Evening _____

Job Search/Marketing Ideas

_____
_____
_____
_____
_____
_____
_____

To Mail or Ship

_____
_____

Secretarial/Printing

_____
_____
_____
_____

Pending

_____
_____
_____
_____
_____

Today's 3 Accomplishments

_____
_____
_____
_____
_____

It's okay to be nervous. Just try to do it like a duck: calm on the surface and paddling like hell underneath.

—HARRY R. NEVLING,
SPHR, President, American Society
Healthcare Human Resources Association (ASHHRA)

Notes

Copyright 1993 Tom Cheney. Reprinted with permission.

"It happens . . . just take a few moments, relax, collect your thoughts and I'm sure your name will come to you."

59
Interviewing

WE FORFEIT THREE-FOURTHS OF OURSELVES TO BE LIKE OTHER PEOPLE.

—ARTHUR SCHOPENHAUER

Today's Day and Date

To Do Checklist—Action Today

"A" Prospects

Meetings/Appointments/Interviews

7:00 AM

8:00

9:00

10:00

11:00

12:00 PM

1:00

2:00

3:00

4:00

5:00

Evening

Job Search/Marketing Ideas

To Mail or Ship

Secretarial/Printing

Pending

Today's 3 Accomplishments

124

THE JOB SEARCH TIME MANAGER

I dislike a candidate who tries to be too perfect—who tries to hide behind their "mask."

—RICHARD J. MASEK,
Director,
Affiliated Personnel Advisors

Notes

Copyright 1993 Tom Cheney. Reprinted with permission.

"I must say, I'm particularly impressed with the coffee rings and eraser crumbs on your resume."

THE BEST WAY TO PREDICT THE FUTURE IS TO PLAN IT.

—PETER DRUCKER

Today's Day and Date
_____

To Do Checklist—Action Today
_____
_____
_____
_____

"A" Prospects
_____
_____

Meetings/Appointments/Interviews

7:00 AM _____
_____

8:00 _____
_____

9:00 _____
_____

10:00 _____
_____

11:00 _____
_____

12:00 PM _____
_____

1:00 _____
_____

2:00 _____
_____

3:00 _____
_____

4:00 _____
_____

5:00 _____
_____

Evening _____
_____

Job Search/Marketing Ideas
_____
_____
_____
_____
_____
_____
_____

To Mail or Ship
_____
_____
_____

Secretarial/Printing
_____
_____
_____
_____

Pending
_____
_____
_____
_____

Today's 3 Accomplishments
_____
_____
_____
_____
_____
_____

We're impressed by candidates who take self-development steps on their own time.

—JANET BURKARD,
Director of People Development,
Cellular One

Notes

Les Moore by Phillip Jewell

Copyright 1993 Phillip Jewell. Reprinted with permission.

"Good evening, and welcome to Night School."

Keep true to the dreams of thy youth.

—FERDINAND SCHILLER

Today's Day and Date

To Do Checklist—Action Today

_____
_____
_____

"A" Prospects

_____
_____

Meetings/Appointments/Interviews

7:00 AM _____

8:00 _____

9:00 _____

10:00 _____

11:00 _____

12:00 PM _____

1:00 _____

2:00 _____

3:00 _____

4:00 _____

5:00 _____

Evening _____

Job Search/Marketing Ideas

_____
_____
_____
_____
_____
_____
_____

To Mail or Ship

_____
_____

Secretarial/Printing

_____
_____
_____
_____

Pending

_____
_____
_____
_____
_____

Today's 3 Accomplishments

_____
_____
_____
_____
_____
_____
_____

Make me think this job is the culmination of your career goals, but don't overdo it.

—RICHARD S. MACK,
Director of Personnel,
U.S. Olympic Committee

Notes

POT-SHOTS NO. 2257.

**IF YOU WANT
TO START
AT THE TOP
OF YOUR
PROFESSION,**

INVENT
YOUR OWN
PROFESSION.

Ashleigh
Brilliant

Reprinted with permission.

LIFE IS EITHER AN EXCITING ADVENTURE OR IT IS NOTHING.

—HELEN KELLER

Today's Day and Date

_____

To Do Checklist—Action Today

_____
_____
_____
_____

"A" Prospects

_____
_____
_____

Meetings/Appointments/Interviews

7:00 AM _____
_____
8:00 _____
_____
9:00 _____
_____
10:00 _____
_____
11:00 _____
_____
12:00 PM _____
_____
1:00 _____
_____
2:00 _____
_____
3:00 _____
_____
4:00 _____
_____
5:00 _____
_____
Evening _____

Job Search/Marketing Ideas

_____
_____
_____
_____
_____
_____
_____

To Mail or Ship

_____
_____
_____

Secretarial/Printing

_____
_____
_____
_____
_____

Pending

_____
_____
_____
_____
_____

Today's 3 Accomplishments

_____
_____
_____
_____
_____
_____

130

Always try to ask questions first so you can find out what the company needs and then show how you fit the bill. Probe the interviewer about her/his life— find as much common ground as possible. Build rapport at the start of the interview.

—RICHARD J. MASEK,
Director,
Affiliated Personnel Advisors

Notes

HERMAN

PERSONNEL

©1976 Universal Press Syndicate

Herman copyright Jim Unger. Reprinted with permission of Universal Press Syndicate. All rights reserved.

"Night work! You mean when it's dark?"

63
Interviewing

Never permit a dichotomy to rule your life, a dichotomy in which you hate what you do so you can have pleasure in your spare time. Look for a situation in which your work will give you as much happiness as your spare time.

—EDWARD L. BERNAYS

Today's Day and Date

_____

To Do Checklist—Action Today

_____
_____
_____
_____

"A" Prospects

_____
_____
_____

Meetings/Appointments/Interviews

7:00 AM _____
_____

8:00 _____

9:00 _____

10:00 _____

11:00 _____

12:00 PM _____

1:00 _____

2:00 _____

3:00 _____

4:00 _____

5:00 _____

Evening _____
_____

Job Search/Marketing Ideas

_____
_____
_____
_____
_____
_____
_____
_____

To Mail or Ship

_____
_____

Secretarial/Printing

_____
_____
_____
_____

Pending

_____
_____
_____
_____

Today's 3 Accomplishments

_____
_____
_____
_____
_____
_____

THE QUICKEST WAY TO END MY COMMITMENT TO THE INTERVIEW IS TO EMBELLISH YOUR SKILLS AND KNOWLEDGE BEYOND REALITY.

—RICHARD S. MACK,
Director of Personnel,
U.S. Olympic Committee

Notes

HERMAN®

"I can only say I'll let you know. I have another four hundred applicants to see."

WE BECOME WHAT WE THINK ABOUT.

—EARL NIGHTENGALE

Today's Day and Date

_____

To Do Checklist—Action Today

_____
_____
_____
_____

"A" Prospects

_____
_____

Meetings/Appointments/Interviews

7:00 AM _____
_____

8:00 _____
_____

9:00 _____
_____

10:00 _____
_____

11:00 _____
_____

12:00 PM _____
_____

1:00 _____
_____

2:00 _____
_____

3:00 _____
_____

4:00 _____
_____

5:00 _____
_____

Evening _____
_____

Job Search/Marketing Ideas

_____
_____
_____
_____
_____
_____
_____

To Mail or Ship

_____
_____
_____

Secretarial/Printing

_____
_____
_____
_____
_____

Pending

_____
_____
_____
_____

Today's 3 Accomplishments

_____
_____
_____
_____
_____
_____

Try to understand the issues, concerns, opportunities facing the company and be able to sell the "value added" you will bring.

—JAMES L. RASMUS,
Director Sales Support,
JI Case, International Business Group

Notes

the neighborhood.

NOW, IF I COULD JUST FIGURE OUT HOW I REALLY FEEL, AS OPPOSED TO HOW I THINK I'M SUPPOSED TO FEEL...

5-7
© 1990 by Cowles Syndicate, Inc.

Reprinted with special permission of King Features Syndicate.

Deep thinking screws up another perfectly nice day.

135

NEVER BELIEVE IN NEVER.

—ROBERT SCHULLER

Today's Day and Date

To Do Checklist—Action Today

"A" Prospects

Meetings/Appointments/Interviews

7:00 AM

8:00

9:00

10:00

11:00

12:00 PM

1:00

2:00

3:00

4:00

5:00

Evening

Job Search/Marketing Ideas

To Mail or Ship

Secretarial/Printing

Pending

Today's 3 Accomplishments

Above all, demonstrate confidence and a "can do" attitude.

—SCOTT G. HOWARD,
President,
Reid Merrill Brunson & Associates

Notes

STEIN

Copyright 1993 Eli Stein. Reprinted with permission.

66
Interviewing

The most persuasive person in the world is the man or woman who has a fanatical belief in an idea, a product or service.

—CAVETT ROBERT

Today's Day and Date	Job Search/Marketing Ideas
To Do Checklist—Action Today	
"A" Prospects	
	To Mail or Ship
Meetings/Appointments/Interviews	
7:00 AM	Secretarial/Printing
8:00	
9:00	
10:00	
11:00	Pending
12:00 PM	
1:00	
2:00	
3:00	Today's 3 Accomplishments
4:00	
5:00	
Evening	

NEVER UNDERESTIMATE THE NEED TO "SELL" YOURSELF RATHER THAN SIMPLY PROVIDING DATA ABOUT YOURSELF.

—JENNIFER CRAIG,
Executive Vice President,
Reid Merrill Brunson & Associates

Notes

Copyright 1993 Tom Cheney. Reprinted with permission.

"Yes, you are the aggressive sales type we're looking for . . . no, I don't want to buy your briefcase."

BUILD A DREAM AND THE DREAM WILL BUILD YOU.

—ROBERT SCHULLER

Today's Day and Date
_____

To Do Checklist—Action Today
_____
_____
_____
_____

"A" Prospects
_____
_____

Meetings/Appointments/Interviews

7:00 AM _____
_____

8:00 _____
_____

9:00 _____
_____

10:00 _____
_____

11:00 _____
_____

12:00 PM _____
_____

1:00 _____
_____

2:00 _____
_____

3:00 _____
_____

4:00 _____
_____

5:00 _____
_____

Evening _____
_____

Job Search/Marketing Ideas
_____
_____
_____
_____
_____
_____
_____
_____

To Mail or Ship
_____
_____

Secretarial/Printing
_____
_____
_____
_____
_____

Pending
_____
_____
_____
_____

Today's 3 Accomplishments
_____
_____
_____
_____
_____
_____

Be positive and friendly, never phony, in your responses.

—LEO E. PERINO,
Director HR & FM,
Western Farm Bureau Life Insurance

Notes

Copyright 1993 Tom Cheney. Reprinted with permission.

"Are you sure you don't want to change your story about your previous experience?"

*THE VOYAGE OF THE BEST
SHIP IS A ZIGZAG LINE
OF A HUNDRED TACKS.*

—RALPH WALDO EMERSON

Today's Day and Date

_____

To Do Checklist—Action Today

_____
_____
_____

"A" Prospects

_____
_____
_____

Meetings/Appointments/Interviews

7:00 AM _____

8:00 _____

9:00 _____

10:00 _____

11:00 _____

12:00 PM _____

1:00 _____

2:00 _____

3:00 _____

4:00 _____

5:00 _____

Evening _____

Job Search/Marketing Ideas

_____
_____
_____
_____
_____
_____

To Mail or Ship

_____
_____

Secretarial/Printing

_____
_____
_____
_____

Pending

_____
_____
_____
_____

Today's 3 Accomplishments

_____
_____
_____
_____

142

Show you've researched my organization by asking questions that only someone highly knowledgeable would be able to ask.

—RICHARD S. MACK,
Director of Personnel,
U.S. Olympic Committee

Notes

"Yes, we do have an affirmative-action program, but it doesn't cover right-brained people."

*CHARACTER IS THE ABILITY TO
CARRY OUT A GOOD RESOLUTION
LONG AFTER THE MOOD IN WHICH IT
WAS MADE HAS LEFT YOU.*

—CAVETT ROBERT

Today's Day and Date

To Do Checklist—Action Today

"A" Prospects

Meetings/Appointments/Interviews

7:00 AM

8:00

9:00

10:00

11:00

12:00 PM

1:00

2:00

3:00

4:00

5:00

Evening

Job Search/Marketing Ideas

To Mail or Ship

Secretarial/Printing

Pending

Today's 3 Accomplishments

IN A RECRUITING INTERVIEW, THERE ARE RARELY "RIGHT" OR "WRONG" ANSWERS TO DIFFICULT QUESTIONS. I AM USUALLY EVALUATING THE CHARACTER OF AN INDIVIDUAL UNDER PRESSURE.

—GUY BENNETT,
Personnel Manager,
Schlumberger

Notes

"Sorry . . . perhaps that question was a bit personal."

The mark of the mature person is that their living is integrated around self-chosen goals.

—ROLLO MAY

Today's Day and Date

Job Search/Marketing Ideas

To Do Checklist—Action Today

"A" Prospects

To Mail or Ship

Meetings/Appointments/Interviews

7:00 AM

8:00

9:00

Secretarial/Printing

10:00

11:00

Pending

12:00 PM

1:00

2:00

3:00

Today's 3 Accomplishments

4:00

5:00

Evening

146

FOR A MANAGEMENT POSITION, MAKE SURE I KNOW YOU ARE A LEADER AND A DEVELOPER OF PEOPLE—NOT JUST A MANAGER.

—RICHARD S. MACK,
Director of Personnel,
U.S. Olympic Committee

Notes

Reprinted with permission.

"This is a high-stress position, so you'll be expected to maintain an ulcer."

147

What your heart thinks great, is great. The soul's emphasis is always right.

—RALPH WALDO EMERSON

Today's Day and Date	Job Search/Marketing Ideas
To Do Checklist—Action Today	
"A" Prospects	
	To Mail or Ship
Meetings/Appointments/Interviews	
7:00 AM	
	Secretarial/Printing
8:00	
9:00	
10:00	
11:00	Pending
12:00 PM	
1:00	
2:00	
	Today's 3 Accomplishments
3:00	
4:00	
5:00	
Evening	

ANY APPLICANT WHO DOES NOT HAVE A GOOD LIST OF QUESTIONS SEEMS UNPREPARED.

—SHARON ALMIRALL,
Marketing Director,
Duluth News-Tribune

Notes

Copyright 1993 Eli Stein. Reprinted with permission.

"I hope you don't mind—I brought my own set of questions for you to ask me."

To be nobody—but yourself—in a world that is doing its best, night and day, to make you everybody else—means to fight the hardest battle which any human being can fight.

—E.E. CUMMINGS

Today's Day and Date

_____

To Do Checklist—Action Today

_____
_____
_____
_____

"A" Prospects

_____
_____

Meetings/Appointments/Interviews

7:00 AM _____
_____
8:00 _____
_____
9:00 _____
_____
10:00 _____
_____
11:00 _____
_____
12:00 PM _____
_____
1:00 _____
_____
2:00 _____
_____
3:00 _____
_____
4:00 _____
_____
5:00 _____
_____
Evening _____

Job Search/Marketing Ideas

_____
_____
_____
_____
_____
_____
_____

To Mail or Ship

_____
_____

Secretarial/Printing

_____
_____
_____
_____

Pending

_____
_____
_____
_____

Today's 3 Accomplishments

_____
_____
_____
_____
_____
_____
_____

IF YOU DON'T KNOW THE ANSWER TO A QUESTION, DON'T TRY TO FAKE A RESPONSE.

—DAVID A. SWAN,
VP Human Resources,
Leprino Foods

Notes

HONESTY
IS THE BEST
IMAGE

1-4

Tom Wilson

73
Interviewing

The creation of genius begins when each of us takes an inner dream and makes the vision real by risking to give it form.

—DAVID VISCOTT, M.D.

Today's Day and Date

To Do Checklist—Action Today

"A" Prospects

Meetings/Appointments/Interviews

7:00 AM

8:00

9:00

10:00

11:00

12:00 PM

1:00

2:00

3:00

4:00

5:00

Evening

Job Search/Marketing Ideas

To Mail or Ship

Secretarial/Printing

Pending

Today's 3 Accomplishments

You'll sell yourself best by being honest, being consistent, and being yourself.

—ROY J. WILSON,
Sr. V.P. Human Resources,
Pearle Vision

Notes

"Oh, I have lots of previous experience. Would you like to see a videotape of me working?"

HARD WORK IS WORK WITHOUT LOVE.

—JERRY GILLIES

Today's Day and Date

To Do Checklist—Action Today

"A" Prospects

Meetings/Appointments/Interviews

7:00 AM

8:00

9:00

10:00

11:00

12:00 PM

1:00

2:00

3:00

4:00

5:00

Evening

Job Search/Marketing Ideas

To Mail or Ship

Secretarial/Printing

Pending

Today's 3 Accomplishments

Decision makers have accepted poor answers to important questions— and still hired the candidate— because they liked him or her so much.

—BETSY MCGEE,
Career Consultant, The McGee Group

Notes

Copyright 1993 H.L. Schwadron. Reprinted with permission.

"Very well, Mr. Potter, I blinked first. You're hired."

You will recognize your own path when you come upon it, because you will suddenly have all the energy and imagination you will ever need.

—JERRY GILLIES

Today's Day and Date _____

To Do Checklist—Action Today

_____
_____
_____
_____

"A" Prospects

_____
_____

Meetings/Appointments/Interviews

7:00 AM _____
_____

8:00 _____
_____

9:00 _____
_____

10:00 _____
_____

11:00 _____
_____

12:00 PM _____
_____

1:00 _____
_____

2:00 _____
_____

3:00 _____
_____

4:00 _____
_____

5:00 _____
_____

Evening _____
_____

Job Search/Marketing Ideas

_____
_____
_____
_____
_____
_____
_____

To Mail or Ship

_____
_____

Secretarial/Printing

_____
_____
_____
_____

Pending

_____
_____
_____
_____

Today's 3 Accomplishments

_____
_____
_____
_____

YOU KNOW YOUR SELF-ESTEEM IS OPTIMAL WHEN YOU EMERGE FROM AN INTERVIEW MENTALLY CONGRATULATING YOURSELF ON BEING SO DAMN GOOD!

—KERRI S. SMITH,
Careers Reporter,
The Rocky Mountain News

Notes

_____
_____
_____
_____
_____
_____
_____
_____
_____
_____
_____
_____
_____
_____
_____
_____
_____
_____
_____
_____
_____
_____
_____

FRANK & ERNEST® by Bob Thaves

FRANK & ERNEST reprinted by permission of NEA, Inc.

REAL SATISFACTION COMES FROM . . .
TOTAL EFFORT FULLY EXPENDED
IN QUEST OF A WORTHY IDEA.

—Zig Ziglar

Today's Day and Date	Job Search/Marketing Ideas
To Do Checklist—Action Today	
"A" Prospects	
	To Mail or Ship
Meetings/Appointments/Interviews	
7:00 AM	
	Secretarial/Printing
8:00	
9:00	
10:00	
11:00	Pending
12:00 PM	
1:00	
2:00	
3:00	Today's 3 Accomplishments
4:00	
5:00	
Evening	

Ask for the job very assertively at the end of the interview (if you are interested, of course).

—RICHARD J. MASEK,
Director,
Affiliated Personnel Advisors

Notes

"I make it a point to hire ex-Air Force personnel. I like employees who salute!"

159

Living is a form of not being sure, not knowing what next or how. The moment you know how, you begin to die a little.

—AGNES DE MILLE

Today's Day and Date
_____

To Do Checklist—Action Today
_____
_____
_____
_____

"A" Prospects
_____
_____

Meetings/Appointments/Interviews

7:00 AM _____

8:00 _____

9:00 _____

10:00 _____

11:00 _____

12:00 PM _____

1:00 _____

2:00 _____

3:00 _____

4:00 _____

5:00 _____

Evening _____

Job Search/Marketing Ideas
_____
_____
_____
_____
_____
_____
_____

To Mail or Ship
_____
_____

Secretarial/Printing
_____
_____
_____
_____
_____

Pending
_____
_____
_____
_____

Today's 3 Accomplishments
_____
_____
_____
_____

Take notes in the interview. Summarize the company's needs and your potential contribution, as well as a plan to shore up deficiencies if hired. Formalize in a letter to the hiring manager.

—JENNIFER CRAIG,
Executive Vice President,
Reid Merrill Brunson & Associates

Notes

"I'll have the personnel manager's lunch and he'll have the job applicant's lunch."

THE BIGGEST MISTAKE PEOPLE MAKE IN LIFE IS NOT TRYING TO MAKE A LIVING AT DOING WHAT THEY MOST ENJOY.

—MALCOLM FORBES

Today's Day and Date

_____

To Do Checklist—Action Today

_____
_____
_____

"A" Prospects

_____
_____
_____

Meetings/Appointments/Interviews

7:00 AM _____
_____
8:00 _____
_____
9:00 _____
_____
10:00 _____
_____
11:00 _____
_____
12:00 PM _____
_____
1:00 _____
_____
2:00 _____
_____
3:00 _____
_____
4:00 _____
_____
5:00 _____
_____

Evening _____
_____

Job Search/Marketing Ideas

_____
_____
_____
_____
_____
_____

To Mail or Ship

_____
_____

Secretarial/Printing

_____
_____
_____
_____

Pending

_____
_____
_____
_____

Today's 3 Accomplishments

_____
_____
_____
_____
_____
_____
_____

Follow up with a handwritten thank you the same day to each person you talked with. Don't forget the receptionist. He or she often gives very valuable advice to the "deciding" manager.

—LEO E. PERINO,
Director HR & FM,
Western Farm Bureau Life Insurance

Notes

© ASHLEIGH BRILLIANT 1985.   POT-SHOTS NO. 3938.

THERE PROBABLY IS AN EASY ROAD TO SUCCESS~

THE TROUBLE IS, IT'S VERY HARD TO FIND.

Reprinted with permission.

THOSE WHO BELIEVE THE MOST ALWAYS GET THE MOST.

—ERNEST HOLMES

Today's Day and Date

To Do Checklist—Action Today

_____
_____
_____
_____

"A" Prospects

_____
_____

Meetings/Appointments/Interviews

7:00 AM _____

8:00 _____

9:00 _____

10:00 _____

11:00 _____

12:00 PM _____

1:00 _____

2:00 _____

3:00 _____

4:00 _____

5:00 _____

Evening _____

Job Search/Marketing Ideas

_____
_____
_____
_____
_____
_____

To Mail or Ship

_____
_____

Secretarial/Printing

_____
_____
_____

Pending

_____
_____
_____
_____

Today's 3 Accomplishments

_____
_____
_____
_____
_____

I'm impressed by someone who calls back expressing enthusiasm about the job and additional contributions they can make.

—JENNIFER CRAIG,
Executive Vice President,
Reid Merrill Brunson & Associates

Notes

"We've got lots of self-starters. We need some self-finishers."

You always pass failure on the way to success.

—MICKEY ROONEY

Today's Day and Date	Job Search/Marketing Ideas
To Do Checklist—Action Today	
"A" Prospects	To Mail or Ship
Meetings/Appointments/Interviews	
7:00 AM	Secretarial/Printing
8:00	
9:00	
10:00	
11:00	Pending
12:00 PM	
1:00	
2:00	Today's 3 Accomplishments
3:00	
4:00	
5:00	
Evening	

80
Disappointment

MAINTAIN BALANCE IN YOUR SEARCH: EXERCISE, FAMILY, PERSONAL GROWTH AND A HOPEFUL SPIRIT.

—WILLIAM H. HECK,
VP Human Resources,
HCA Wesley Medical Center

Notes

HERMAN®

5/10

"Will you please mind your own business and sit somewhere else? I've had a very rough day."

81
Disappointment

The story of the pump is the story of life. If you pump long enough, hard enough and enthusiastically enough, sooner or later the effort will bring forth the reward.

—ZIG ZIGLAR

Today's Day and Date
_____

To Do Checklist—Action Today
_____
_____
_____

"A" Prospects
_____
_____

Meetings/Appointments/Interviews

7:00 AM _____
_____

8:00 _____
_____

9:00 _____
_____

10:00 _____
_____

11:00 _____
_____

12:00 PM _____
_____

1:00 _____
_____

2:00 _____
_____

3:00 _____
_____

4:00 _____
_____

5:00 _____
_____

Evening _____
_____

Job Search/Marketing Ideas
_____
_____
_____
_____
_____
_____

To Mail or Ship
_____
_____
_____

Secretarial/Printing
_____
_____
_____
_____

Pending
_____
_____
_____
_____

Today's 3 Accomplishments
_____
_____
_____
_____
_____
_____

DON'T QUIT LOOKING WHEN YOU'RE TIRED OR DISCOURAGED; YOU'LL HAVE PLENTY OF TIME TO REST ONCE YOU HAVE A JOB.

—JAMES D. COLLINS,
VP Finance, XEL Communications

Notes

FRANK & ERNEST® by Bob Thaves

FRANK & ERNEST reprinted by permission of NEA, Inc.

169

WINNING IS NOT EVERYTHING, BUT THE EFFORT TO WIN IS.

—ZIG ZIGLAR

Today's Day and Date
_____

To Do Checklist—Action Today
_____
_____
_____
_____

"A" Prospects
_____
_____

Meetings/Appointments/Interviews

7:00 AM _____
_____

8:00 _____
_____

9:00 _____
_____

10:00 _____
_____

11:00 _____
_____

12:00 PM _____
_____

1:00 _____
_____

2:00 _____
_____

3:00 _____
_____

4:00 _____
_____

5:00 _____
_____

Evening _____

Job Search/Marketing Ideas
_____
_____
_____
_____
_____
_____
_____
_____

To Mail or Ship
_____
_____

Secretarial/Printing
_____
_____
_____
_____

Pending
_____
_____
_____
_____

Today's 3 Accomplishments
_____
_____
_____
_____
_____
_____

The job hunters' major problem is that they don't keep on keeping on.

—BETSY McGEE,
Career Consultant, The McGee Group

Notes

© ASHLEIGH BRILLIANT 1985.   POT-SHOTS NO. 3941.

I'LL PUT IT DOWN IMMEDIATELY,

ON MY LIST OF THINGS TO POSTPONE.

Ashleigh Brilliant

Reprinted with permission.

171

Try to be cheerful even when you're not happy. Cheerfulness is more under our control than happiness. A moderate amount of denial can be healthy. When you're discouraged, you often can change your mood if you act enthusiastic—as optimists often do instinctively because they don't want to drag down the energy of the people around them.

—ALAN LOY McGINNIS,
Author, *The Power of Optimism*

Today's Day and Date

To Do Checklist—Action Today

"A" Prospects

Meetings/Appointments/Interviews

7:00 AM

8:00

9:00

10:00

11:00

12:00 PM

1:00

2:00

3:00

4:00

5:00

Evening

Job Search/Marketing Ideas

To Mail or Ship

Secretarial/Printing

Pending

Today's 3 Accomplishments

IF YOU DON'T MAINTAIN
A GOOD ATTITUDE IN YOUR
JOB SEARCH, HOW DO I KNOW
YOU'LL HAVE A GOOD ATTITUDE
IN YOUR JOB?

—JAMES D. COLLINS,
VP Finance,
XEL Communications

Notes

"It all happened so fast . . . the interview was going well, some pressure, but not enough to make me sweat, then all of a sudden I heard myself saying, 'Hire me, or I'll kill you.'"

173

Fall seven times, stand up eight.

—JAPANESE PROVERB

Today's Day and Date	**Job Search/Marketing Ideas**
To Do Checklist—Action Today	
"A" Prospects	
	To Mail or Ship
Meetings/Appointments/Interviews	
7:00 AM	
	Secretarial/Printing
8:00	
9:00	
10:00	
11:00	**Pending**
12:00 PM	
1:00	
2:00	**Today's 3 Accomplishments**
3:00	
4:00	
5:00	
Evening	

A champion is someone who goes so far they can't go another inch— then goes that inch.

—G.R. "BUZZ" SULLIVAN,
Diving Coach

Notes

Les Moore™ by Phillip Jewell

Copyright 1993 Phillip Jewell. Reprinted with permission.

YOU NEVER REALLY LOSE UNTIL YOU QUIT TRYING.

—MIKE DITKA

Today's Day and Date	Job Search/Marketing Ideas
To Do Checklist—Action Today	
"A" Prospects	To Mail or Ship
Meetings/Appointments/Interviews	
7:00 AM	Secretarial/Printing
8:00	
9:00	
10:00	
11:00	Pending
12:00 PM	
1:00	
2:00	Today's 3 Accomplishments
3:00	
4:00	
5:00	
Evening	

If you don't get the job, realize that 95% of resumes don't even get an interview— YOU'RE STILL OK!

—BETTY HATCHER,
Human Resources Representative,
Penrose Hospital

Notes

Copyright 1993 Eli Stein. Reprinted with permission.

"This is really a very impressive chronological resume, but unfortunately today I'm hiring only from functional resumes."

THE OBJECTIVE IS TO WIN—FAIRLY, SQUARELY, DECENTLY, BY THE RULES—BUT TO WIN.

—VINCE LOMBARDI

Today's Day and Date

To Do Checklist—Action Today

"A" Prospects

Meetings/Appointments/Interviews

7:00 AM

8:00

9:00

10:00

11:00

12:00 PM

1:00

2:00

3:00

4:00

5:00

Evening

Job Search/Marketing Ideas

To Mail or Ship

Secretarial/Printing

Pending

Today's 3 Accomplishments

When negotiating an employment package, convert everything to dollars. It makes maneuvering easier.

—PAUL F. SHADDOCK,
Vice President Human Resources,
United Technologies Microelectronics Center

Notes

Les Moore by Phillip Jewell

Copyright 1993 Phillip Jewell. Reprinted with permission.

"Of course, your figures may vary."

87
Salary

YOU CAN NEVER PLAN THE FUTURE BY THE PAST.

—EDMUND BURKE

Today's Day and Date	Job Search/Marketing Ideas
To Do Checklist—Action Today	
"A" Prospects	To Mail or Ship
Meetings/Appointments/Interviews	
7:00 AM	Secretarial/Printing
8:00	
9:00	
10:00	
11:00	Pending
12:00 PM	
1:00	
2:00	Today's 3 Accomplishments
3:00	
4:00	
5:00	
Evening	

The worst mistake in negotiating salary is to bring it up "early and often."

—ALFRED E. LOPUS,
Manager, Rocky Mountain Region,
The Wyatt Company

Notes

Copyright 1993 Eli Stein. Reprinted with permission.

"We're looking for an action-oriented and growth-oriented individual who is not too salary-oriented."

88
Salary

The assertive person is one who:
1) asks for more,
2) expects more, and
3) gets more.

—BILL GORE

Today's Day and Date
_____

To Do Checklist—Action Today
_____
_____
_____
_____

"A" Prospects
_____
_____

Meetings/Appointments/Interviews

7:00 AM _____

8:00 _____

9:00 _____

10:00 _____

11:00 _____

12:00 PM _____

1:00 _____

2:00 _____

3:00 _____

4:00 _____

5:00 _____

Evening _____

Job Search/Marketing Ideas
_____
_____
_____
_____
_____
_____
_____

To Mail or Ship
_____
_____

Secretarial/Printing
_____
_____
_____
_____

Pending
_____
_____
_____
_____

Today's 3 Accomplishments
_____
_____
_____
_____
_____
_____

If you defer salary discussions until after the company expresses a strong desire to hire you, the bulk of negotiating leverage is in your back pocket.

—WILLIAM A. RECTOR,
President, MicroLithics

Notes

"We're not very big on salary increases, but the size of your office will expand annually."

89
Job Offer

THINK. PRAY. TRUST. THEN DECIDE WITHOUT FEAR.

—Robert Schuller

Today's Day and Date

To Do Checklist—Action Today

_____
_____
_____
_____

"A" Prospects

_____
_____

Meetings/Appointments/Interviews

7:00 AM _____

8:00 _____

9:00 _____

10:00 _____

11:00 _____

12:00 PM _____

1:00 _____

2:00 _____

3:00 _____

4:00 _____

5:00 _____

Evening _____

Job Search/Marketing Ideas

_____
_____
_____
_____
_____
_____

To Mail or Ship

_____
_____

Secretarial/Printing

_____
_____
_____
_____

Pending

_____
_____
_____
_____

Today's 3 Accomplishments

_____
_____
_____
_____
_____

*In the '90s
you are either overworked
or unemployed.*

—JOY SANDBERG,
Director of Research,
Mountain States Employer's Council

Notes

Les Moore by Phillip Jewell

Copyright 1993 Phillip Jewell. Reprinted with permission.

"Can you believe it? They gave me my own office."

185

KEEP YOUR
RESUME LOCKED,
LOADED, AND READY
TO FIRE AT ALL TIMES.

—Harvey Mackay,
Author, *Sharkproof*

Today's Day and Date

_____

To Do Checklist—Action Today

_____
_____
_____

"A" Prospects

_____
_____

Meetings/Appointments/Interviews

7:00 AM _____

8:00 _____

9:00 _____

10:00 _____

11:00 _____

12:00 PM _____

1:00 _____

2:00 _____

3:00 _____

4:00 _____

5:00 _____

Evening _____

Job Search/Marketing Ideas

_____
_____
_____
_____
_____
_____
_____

To Mail or Ship

_____
_____

Secretarial/Printing

_____
_____
_____
_____

Pending

_____
_____
_____
_____

Today's 3 Accomplishments

_____
_____
_____
_____
_____
_____

In the business world today, job security could be your ability to find another job right away.

—HARVEY H. SIMS,
Director, Organization Development,
CoBANK

Notes

Copyright 1993 Eli Stein. Reprinted with permission.

"Henderson! Get back to the office immediately."

Frequently Called Numbers

Name	Spouse	Company	Home Phone	Work Phone	Notes
SAMPLE Bob Arisman	Cindy	Search Group	303-555-7572	303-555-1434	Recruiter

THE
JOB
SEARCH
TIME
MANAGER

First Name	
Last Name	
Title	
Company	
Street	
City/State	
Zip	
Salutation	
BPhone	
FAX	
Mobile/Pager	
HPhone	
CODE	
Notes	

First Name	
Last Name	
Title	
Company	
Street	
City/State	
Zip	
Salutation	
BPhone	
FAX	
Mobile/Pager	
HPhone	
CODE	
Notes	

First Name	
Last Name	
Title	
Company	
Street	
City/State	
Zip	
Salutation	
BPhone	
FAX	
Mobile/Pager	
HPhone	
CODE	
Notes	

Label 18 file folders with the headings below, or create these files in your computer. Review all records daily for a few weeks until you feel comfortable with them. This system will make your job hunting life much easier:

1. *"A" Prospects.* A list of the "hot ones" you don't want to forget. Include name, company, telephone number, and status. Check this list daily.

2. *Add to Network.* Names, addresses and telephone numbers you want to add to your database.

3. *Company Names.* Make a folder for each key prospect company. For example: Compaq, DEC, IBM. Insert notes from meetings, follow-up letters, and library research.

4. *Hold.* Maps, directions to meetings, anything you may need later, but not on a specific date. (Everything associated with a specific date goes into the follow-up file, described later.)

5. *Hunches.* Clippings of news stories suggesting job opportunities: plant openings, new product announcements, company growth, promotions, mergers. Consider three folders: a) *Local Hunches*, b) *Regional Hunches*, and c) *National Hunches*.

6. *Ideas/Strategies.* Any brainstorm you get that could help you later. Example: "To reach hiring manager, call early a.m. or late p.m. before the secretary arrives, or after she leaves." If you get a letter with a business reply card in it and decide to try something similar, the card goes into your *Ideas* file.

7. *Junk Mail.* Letters and marketing pieces that could be adapted for the job search. If your insurance agent sends you a friendly letter and you want to remember the salutation, save it here.

8. *Marketing Letters.* High-powered letters you plan to use again. Add additional folders for: a) *Friend Letters*, b) *SEARCH Letters*, c) *Thank You Letters*, d) *Want Ad Letters*, and e) *Reference Letters*.

9. *Meeting Announcements.* Brochures or clippings describing conferences, conventions, business meetings.

10. *No Interest Now.* Don't throw notes and records away when someone indicates lack of interest. Save and review them in four to six weeks. Things often change. "No" doesn't always mean "never."

11. *Postage.* Stamps in all denominations, especially 29 and 52 cents.

12. *Proposals/Samples.* If employers have asked for proposals describing how you would solve a problem, they are filed here. (Work samples go here too.)

13. *Prospect List.* Companies and individuals that might be of interest. (Also companies that aren't of interest.)

14. *RECAP.* A daily journal of your phone calls and correspondence so you can remember whom you called, what was said, and what you sent.

15. *Resume.* If more than one version, label files *Resume One, Resume Two*, and *Resume Three*.

16. *Send Something.* The names and addresses of people you've promised a letter, a resume, a proposal, a gift, a marketing package, or a thank you note.

17. *Stationery.* Your printed letterhead, envelopes, and business cards.

18. *Telephone Scripts.* Notes to plan for future telephone conversations: what you'll say, what they might say. Answers to key objections. Major accomplishments. Answers to difficult interview questions.

Follow-Up. Get a 9″ × 12″ expanding file numbered 1 to 31 (for the days of the month). Every time you send a letter, decide when you should follow up and put your letter into that slot. A breakfast meeting on the 18th should go into the section marked 18, and so forth. Check the file daily to see what to do. This is an easy way to keep important details from falling through the cracks.

Voice Mail. Make sure your telephone is always answered. Get a telephone answering machine (about $50–100), use an answering service, or subscribe to an electronic voice mailbox (about $13 per month). Some voice mail services give you a new phone number which you can use on letters and resumes as your "office" number, if you're unemployed. Put a businesslike message on your recorder or voice mailbox (no cute messages featuring your kids).

Business/FAX line. If you're based at home, you might want to add a second line for business calls. If your home office line doubles as a FAX line, indicate that on your stationery and correspondence. AT&T has inexpensive residential 800 service that might help if you're relocating. You can keep the number wherever you go. The monthly charge is $5.50 plus a toll for incoming calls. Contact AT&T Signature 800℠ Service at 1-800-327-9700.

Tinker with your tracking system. Customize it to fit your own preferences. Add and delete files. When folders become too thick, or when it takes more than a few seconds to find a document, subdivide files into separate categories. Color code your system using yellow folders for letters, red for resumes, and green for companies.

It's fun to be organized, and being organized will shorten your job search. The organized campaigner gets more done in less time, and thus gets re-employed sooner. The disorganized person can never seem to find his or her notes.

Your next job will probably come either from your friends or from their friends, so networking—building personal relationships—is vitally important.

Where to start. List all your personal friends and business associates. By letter first, then by telephone later, explain your situation, describe your career direction, and ask for advice and ideas.

Reestablish old friendships in follow-up phone calls. Ask about your friend's work and family; get caught up on recent events. Wait until your listener asks about you, then explain your situation in positive terms, even if it's hard to find positives. Ask for suggestions, and specifically ask, "Who else should I be talking to?"

If you find networking hard because you don't want to use your friends, or because you dislike asking for help, overcome this by genuinely caring about those you call. Your interest will delight them, and they'll gladly share information. Remember, you'd willingly help them if they came to you needing similar support.

Force yourself to use the telephone; it gets easier as you call. Look for information about industry trends or trends in your functional area or specialty. Watch for plans for new products or services. Seek out emerging markets, hidden jobs, and companies that are hiring. Listen for upcoming retirements and insider tips about corporate culture or political infighting. Pay attention to news of reorganizations, expansions, mergers or acquisitions. Ask about business associations, publications, or resources. Focus on anything change-related, because change means opportunity.

How to structure a meeting. Your telephone calls will soon produce face-to-face meetings. In the beginning, be friendly and establish rapport. Set the stage by asking how much time you'll have. State your purpose clearly and directly. Share your excitement and enthusiasm, and ask for advice and ideas. In general, listen more than you talk. Watch for opportunities, and take brief notes using the worksheet on page 195. Ask for referrals to other experts. Before you leave, ask for a business card, discuss a next step, and offer heartfelt thanks.

How to recognize opportunities. Don't look only for specific openings where someone else held the job before. Watch closely for:

1. Problems you would *enjoy* solving.

2. Weaknesses in a company where you could help. Example: becoming an in-house attorney where there was none before.

3.   Work groups where you like them and they like you. In employment this is called "good chemistry" or "good fit."

4.   Companies where people are complaining, troubled, or under pressure. This often indicates too few people to do the work at hand: a need for hiring.

5.   Anywhere you see something *missing* that you could add, a logical extension or improvement. Example: pizza *delivery* for a pizza restaurant.

Listen 80% and talk 20%. Personal meetings should be interactive, like tennis; but in general, others would rather talk than listen. Therefore, give them your full attention. Listening builds trust and says, "I care about you." If you're having trouble getting hired, try listening 50% more.

Yet there *is* a time to talk about *yourself.* Sooner or later, your host will say, "Tell me about yourself," "Why are you here?" or "How can I help you?" When that happens, take twenty seconds—not twenty minutes—to answer.

Walk in prepared. Know what you want. Never enter a meeting without knowing why you're there. You'll waste your time, waste your contact's time, and look unprofessional. Show up unprepared too often and word will get around that you lack focus. No one will want to talk to you.

Key questions to ask. One goal of networking is to get referrals, but how do you ask for names? You can be too direct and put others off. You can be too vague, and come away empty handed. So what do you say?

In general, it's better to be subtle and indirect rather than blunt. "Can you give me the names of your friends?" might put your host on the defensive; the answer may be no. "Who else should I be talking to?" is far less threatening and will elicit the names of friends and key contacts anyway.

If you're wondering what else to ask in a networking session, try these on for size:

1.   How does my resume look? What would you change or modify? Are my letters crystal clear?

2.   Do you have any advice or ideas for me?

3.   Who else should I be talking to?

4.   Are there any groups or organizations I should attend?

5.   Are there any books or publications I should read?

6.   What would you do if you were me? Who would you be talking to?

How to end. When appropriate, establish a next step: a phone call, follow-up meeting, something to be mailed. If you end with no next step, you miss the chance to involve this person in your campaign—possibly a big mistake.

THE
JOB
SEARCH
TIME
MANAGER

The Secrets Of Effective Networking

Tell people you value their suggestions and plan to take action on them. Say, for example, "I'll call the people you recommended and read the articles you suggested. Then I'll check back in a week or so to let you know what happened."

This approach lets the person know you take them seriously. It cements the relationship. In addition, it makes this person a more permanent part of your network, not just a passing face. If you handle it right, you can call later for further help.

Don't make the mistake of contacting people only once. Your search will never build momentum. As you meet technical experts and business leaders, become a friend to them, and they'll likely return the friendship.

Your contact network should always be growing, not shrinking. The best way to expand it is to seek out new people and build relationships. It doesn't really matter who you choose, so long as you like them, they like you, and you can help each other.

What to remember. As you launch your job campaign, remember these basics:

⇨ Do your homework; don't expect others to teach what you should research yourself.

⇨ Dress well. Never go into a meeting without checking your appearance in a restroom mirror.

⇨ Seek information only; don't ask directly for a job. Don't be pushy; don't *require* others to help.

⇨ Take brief notes using the worksheet on page 195.

⇨ Be optimistic and upbeat. If you have fun, they'll have fun. If they have fun, they'll like you. If they like you, they're more likely to help you or hire you.

⇨ When someone helps, offer something in return: a book, an article, a favor, or the name of a contact.

⇨ Ask for a business card or for the correct spelling of name, title, and address. Then send a thank you note the same day you talk or meet.

⇨ Always give more than you get.

I once met a highly successful job hunter with a secret. He said, "I create relationships. The relationships create the jobs." He was absolutely right; that's exactly how it works.

Notes From Networking Meeting

THE JOB SEARCH TIME MANAGER

Day and Date:		What I Wore:	
		What They Wore:	
(Get BUSINESS CARDS)			
Main Contact:		Others Who Attended:	
Name		Name	
Title		Title	
Company		Telephone	
City State Zip			
Telephone		Name	
FAX		Title	
Mobile/Pager		Telephone	
Secretary			

Notes:

(Key problems, trends, books or journals to read, upcoming meetings and conferences, things to think about.)

Next Step(s) and Date(s):

1.	2.
3.	4.

Referred to:

Name	Name	Name
Title	Title	Title
Company	Company	Company
City State Zip	City State Zip	City State Zip
Telephone	Telephone	Telephone
FAX	FAX	FAX
Mobile/Pager	Mobile/Pager	Mobile/Pager
Notes	Notes	Notes

THE
JOB
SEARCH
TIME
MANAGER

How To Get A Job Offer

Question:

I get to the second or third interview in the hiring process but can't get a job offer. What could I be doing wrong, and how can I "close the sale?"

Answer:

The fact that you're getting interviews is a good sign. It means that your letters and resume are working and that you're making a good first impression. There are at least eight reasons you could be failing:

1. *You don't look the part.* Your clothing is out of style. Make sure your clothing, including eyewear and briefcase, is current. Have shirts and blouses professionally cleaned and starched.

2. *You lack focus.* You come across as too much of a generalist, as someone who can "do it all"—jack of all trades and master of none. You haven't defined what you want or where you fit, and companies pick that up as lack of direction. Without sharp focus you appear scattered and may come across as a "loose cannon." To combat this, develop strong preferences and be clear about what you want and what you don't want.

3. *You're overselling.* In an attempt to "make the sale" you're pushing too hard, or coming across as desperate. You may appear too eager or over-anxious. Create a high-impact, accomplishment-oriented resume and let it do most of the selling. In general, listen 80% and talk 20% of the time.

4. *Your references are shooting you down.* Who are you using to support your candidacy? Have you asked them what they'll say? Have you prepared guidelines for them? Do they have your resume? Do you brief them before they're called? Be sure to give employers references they can relate to. Engineers like to talk to other engineers, and attorneys prefer other attorneys. Last point: don't overuse your references.

5. *You want too much money.* Don't gauge your present worth on your last salary. The market may have changed; people with your skills could be in oversupply. Do a quick salary survey to determine realistically what you should be earning. Ask what the company plans to pay for the position. Then be flexible. You can lose out by seeming to care more about salary and benefits than about making a big contribution.

6. *You appear difficult.* In multiple interviews companies have time to uncover weaknesses, character flaws, and problem behaviors, such as being arrogant or losing patience. You must appear cooperative, collaborative, and easy to work with.

7. *Someone on the team doesn't like you.* Many companies hire by consensus. That means nearly everyone has to like you. Technical people often feel their track record "speaks for itself," but that's seldom true. In today's team-oriented environment, you need to make a strong effort to be liked by everyone you meet, from entry-level workers to the CEO.

8. *You're not the best qualified.* There may be others who really do fit the job better.

Interviewing is a selling opportunity. It's a relatively short time frame and you're in the spotlight. Even in so-called casual interviews, you're watched and evaluated very closely. You're compared to others and graded. Everything you do, everything you wear, and everything you say is magnified, and either helps or hurts you.

You can sell yourself into a job by using "closing comments." Closing comments are thoughts you drop into the conversation to "close the sale." Closing comments screen you into the position as opposed to screening you out. They say, in effect, "You should hire me. I belong here."

Interviewers want to know at least three things: Are you qualified? Are you motivated? And do you fit into the corporate culture? To be successful, you need to win in all three areas. Let's review them separately.

Are you qualified? The company wants to know if you have the required technical skills and experience. They also want to know if you can take the ball and run with it. You want to show sureness (self confidence) rather than unsureness (lack of confidence). Don't lie, but don't be unnecessarily modest. You want to communicate "I can handle this with no sweat," not, "I could do it if you'd hold my hand every step of the way." Here are some good closing comments:

"The job fits me."
"This would be easy."
"I've done this before."
"I wouldn't have any trouble with that."
"We did a very similar project at AT&T."
"I could make a big contribution in a hurry."
"No problem. That's exactly what we did at AT&T."

Are you motivated? The company wants to know your level of enthusiasm. Do you want the job? If so, how badly? (Remember that wanting it *too badly* can be interpreted as desperation.) Here are some good closing comments:

"I could really see myself fitting in here."
"I think we'd work well together."
"I'd like the job."
"I'd like to take a shot at it."
"I'd love to take charge of this."
"I'd love to give it a try."
"I'd like to get started on it."
"It would be fun to get started."

How do you fit into the corporate culture? The company wants to know if you'll like others and if they'll like you. You want to use phrases that say, in effect, "I like it here." For example:

"I like you people."
"I like what you're doing."
"I like the direction you're taking."
"I like your management philosophy."
"I like what I've seen so far."
"From my perspective, it feels like a great fit."
"I like the way you manage people . . . and I'd like to work for you."

I'm convinced that if you drop these comments into your interview, you'll close the sale and win the job offer.

"If the only tool you have is a hammer, everything begins to look like a nail." Mark Twain.

The principle of the winning edge: "All it takes to win—either over a single competitor or a field of them—is a slight advantage."

Beforehand

- ☐ Recent haircut/styling
- ☐ Starched shirt/blouse
- ☐ New eyeglasses
- ☐ Up-to-date wardrobe

You won't need all the following items. Some may not apply to you, but read through the checklist to be sure you don't forget something vital or show up unprepared.

The Day of Meeting, Take:

- ☐ Appointment book
- ☐ Folder or small briefcase
- ☐ Clean 8½″ × 11″ notepad
- ☐ Your current company literature, job description, and organization chart (if appropriate)
- ☐ Personal compensation history
- ☐ Job shopping list (ideal job design)
- ☐ Six (6) extra resumes
- ☐ Business references (from peers, employers, subordinates, clients, vendors)—either a list of names and addresses, or actual letters of reference
- ☐ Written performance appraisals
- ☐ Memos/letters confirming achievement
- ☐ Photos of you receiving awards (above the 3rd grade)
- ☐ College transcripts (if recent graduate)
- ☐ Facts about prospective employer (clippings, company brochure, annual report, 10K)
- ☐ Questions to ask prospective employer
- ☐ By-line articles (articles you've written)
- ☐ Feature articles (articles written about you)
- ☐ Text of your own past speeches
- ☐ Interview cheat sheet
- ☐ Interview evaluation/comment form
- ☐ Portfolio (non-proprietary samples of your work)—technical drawings, reports, photos (before and after), brochures of products you've sold or developed
- ☐ Chart of experience-match areas (how you fit the job description)

Arrive 15 minutes before your interview. Visit the restroom and check yourself in the mirror. Then be friendly and cordial, but listen 80% and talk 20% unless directly questioned.

Interview Cheat Sheet

Day and Date:

Meeting With:

Name
Title
Company
Address
City State Zip
Telephone
FAX
Mobile/Pager

Major Accomplishments:

1.
2.
3.
4.
5.
6.

Management or Work Style:

1.
2.
3.
4.
5.
6.

Things You Need to Know About Me:

1.
2.
3.
4.
5.

What I Wore:

Reason I Left Last Job:

Answers to Difficult Questions:

1.
2.
3.
4.

My Strengths/Weaknesses:

1.
2.
3.

Questions to Ask Interviewer:

1.
2.
3.
4.
5.
6.

Things I Can Do For You:

1.
2.
3.
4.
5.
6.

Day and Date:		What I Wore:		
		What They Wore:		
Main Contact:		Others Who Attended:		
Name		Name		
Title		Title		
Company		Telephone		
City State Zip				
Telephone		Name		
FAX		Title		
Mobile/Pager		Telephone		
Secretary				

Got Business Cards?   ☐ Yes   ☐ No

Meeting Notes
(General impressions, facts about company, business problems, interviewer's hot buttons, difficult questions, key job requirements, personalities, my selling points, things to do differently next time—and anything else.)

My Performance?   A B C D F

Next Step(s) and Date(s):

1.	2.
3.	4.

Sent Thank You Letter(s)   ☐ Yes (Date/s)   ☐ No

Weekly Scorecard

SUMMARY OF JOB HUNTING ACTIVITIES	SUNDAY	MONDAY	TUESDAY	WEDNESDAY	THURSDAY	FRIDAY	SATURDAY	TOTAL
Phone Calls to Friends								
Phone Calls for Information								
Phone Calls to Recruiters/Agencies								
Phone Calls to Companies/Associations								
Letters/Resumes to Friends								
Letters/Resumes to Want Ads								
Letters/Resumes to Companies								
Thank You Notes/Letters								
Other Letters								
Applications Filled out/Sent								
Breakfasts/Lunches Networking Meetings/ Informational Interviews								
Job Interviews								
Meetings/ Conferences								
Books/Magazine Articles Read								
Other Tactics								
Daily Totals								
Grand Total								

Weekly Record of Job Search Expenses

	SUNDAY	MONDAY	TUESDAY	WEDNESDAY	THURSDAY	FRIDAY	SATURDAY	TOTAL
Day and Date								
Agency Fees								
Auto Mileage								
From/To								
From/To								
From/To								
From/To								
From/To								
From/To								
Book(s), Tape(s), Video(s)								
Career Counseling								
Career Testing								
Directories/Lists								
Dues/Meetings								
Financial/Tax Advice								
Graphic Design								
Legal Fees								
Long Distance Telephone								
Magazines/Journals								
Meals/Entertainment								
Newspapers								
Office Supplies								
Parking								
Postage/FEDEX/UPS								
Printing/Copying								
Secretarial Service								
Seminars/Workshops								
Travel								
Airfare								
Hotel								
Meals								
Car Rental								
Ground Transportation								
Tips								
Other								
Other Expenses								

"People just don't appreciate our ability to nail them."

Keep records of your job hunting expenses, because many of them may be deductible. Deductions are allowed for expenses that are directly related to a search for employment in the same trade or business, regardless of whether the search is successful or unsuccessful.

Job hunting expenses are not deductible if an individual is seeking employment in a new trade or business even if employment is secured. Thus, an individual seeking his or her first job, or switching his or her trade or business, or a person who has been unemployed for such a length of time that there is a substantial lack of continuity to his or her old job, will be denied a deduction.

Always consult a professional tax advisor before claiming specific tax deductions.

1ST QUARTER JANUARY	FEBRUARY	MARCH
2ND QUARTER APRIL	MAY	JUNE
3RD QUARTER JULY	AUGUST	SEPTEMBER
4TH QUARTER OCTOBER	NOVEMBER	DECEMBER

William S. Frank, M.A., Founder and President of **CareerLab**®, a national career counseling firm based in Denver, Colorado. Since 1978 he has been a consultant to the employees, managers, and senior executives of more than 100 major U.S. corporations, including **Ampex, AT&T, Coors, Honeywell, Kaiser-Permanente, Pentax, Schlumberger, Sears Roebuck & Company,** and **TRW.**

Mr. Frank is author of *200 Letters For Job Hunters*, published by **Ten Speed Press**, and he writes "The Career Advisor," a monthly column for **The Colorado Human Resource Association**—a professional organization for personnel managers. His articles have appeared in *The Rocky Mountain News* and *The Wall Street Journal's* "National Business Employment Weekly."

Bill Frank is Executive Producer of the 6-part video series, "Getting FIRED, Getting HIRED: Job Hunting From A to Z." He served three terms as a Board Member of **The Colorado Human Resource Association**—and he makes frequent guest appearances in the media as an expert on career advancement.

CareerLab® is a small team of business experts who provide career advice to individuals and outplacement counseling to corporations. Corporations hire **CareerLab**® to make sure departing employees are re-hired quickly.

CareerLab's® individual clients are typically high-level business executives or professionals—like engineers, lawyers, and CPAs. Their corporate clients span all industries and all geographic locations.

CAREER**L**AB.

9085 East Mineral Circle, Suite 330
Englewood, Colorado 80112
303-790-0505
303-790-0606 FAX
800-723-9675

Craig Lincoln, Director of our Marketing/Communications Group at **CareerLab**®, was the inspiration for this book. He was the driving force behind it; he's its co-creator. As usual, without Craig, we wouldn't have a book.

Thanks to George Young, Christine Carswell, and Hal Hershey at **Ten Speed Press**, for their wisdom, advice, and encouragement. They're the very best.

These artists and cartoonists brought happiness and light into my life; it really was fun living in their world for a few short weeks: Charles Barsotti, Glenn Bernhardt, Ashleigh Brilliant, Tom Cheney, Artemus Cole, Bob Downs, Phillip Jewell, John Louthan, Harley Schwadron, and Eli Stein.

Special thanks to my personal friends, the business experts who provided succinct tidbits of job search advice: Sharon Almirall, Jon Bartoshek, Ed Behlke, Guy Bennett, Linda Bougie, Janet Burkard, Ken Cole, Jim Collins, Jennifer Craig, Bernie Curtis, Alan Forker, Betty Hatcher, Bill Heck, Scott Howard, Bob Junk, Mary Kouri, Cheryl Levitt, Al Lopus, Bob Lundy, Betsy McGee, Rick Mack, Dick Masek, Harry Nevling, Norm Newton, George Ochs, Diane Palmer, Bruce Perch, Leo Perino, Jim Rasmus, Bill Rector, Joy Sandberg, Bob Schulz, Paul Shaddock, Don Shaw, Harv Sims, Kerri Smith, Dave Swan, Kay and Dick Tubbs, Les Woller, and Donita Wolters.

Editorial Cartoonist Ed Stein at the *The Rocky Mountain News* was a great help in securing publishing rights.

I'm grateful to friends in high places who gave permission to use their licensed materials: Kathryn Cohn, Associated Features, Inc.; Jeanne DeSimone, NEA/United Media; Denice Bornander, King Features Syndicate/North America Syndicate; Jim Cavett, Tribune Media Syndicate; and Carla Stiff and Mary Suggett, Universal Press Syndicate. Thanks also to Jim Kennedy, Cavett Robert, Robert Schuller, and Flavia Weedn for the use of their materials.

Cam and Barb Scott, Mitzie Testani and Jeff Mlady at Scott Group, our typesetters, always bring art, beauty, and perfection to their work. It makes a big difference.

My wife, Beverly, is my special friend, and she's given me freedom to be myself, and great support to follow my direction—whatever it might be on any given day. That's a great blessing.

Heartfelt thanks to you all!

LET BILL FRANK HELP YOU
GET A BETTER JOB
FASTER!

200 Letters For Job Hunters

New edition of the world's first and best guidebook for jobhunting by mail. Divided into 20 sections, it covers every possible situation: involving friends, answering want ads, impressing recruiters, cold calling, breaking into new companies, getting good references, following up, rejecting rejection, saying thank you—even asking for a raise. *200 Letters* is packed with new, effective job search tactics and loaded with easy-to-adapt examples that produced interviews and job offers. Save hours, days, weeks of drudgery. Ideal for:

(1) both men and women,
(2) those unemployed or unhappy at work,
(3) all job levels (from entry-level to CEO) in all industries—both public and private sector, and
(4) anyone helping others with career advancement.

Even if you're a non-writer, you'll produce winning letters with this guide!

Paperback, 348 pages
$22.95 (Postage Paid)

Getting FIRED, Getting HIRED:
JOB HUNTING FROM A TO Z

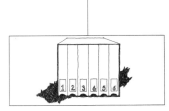

Regardless of what so-called experts say, *job hunting isn't fun and easy.* It's hard work, and simple mistakes can stop you cold. Watch Craig Lincoln navigate every step of a difficult job search. Avoid his mistakes—you'll be hired much more quickly. Besides resume and letter writing, networking, interviewing, and salary negotiation skills, you'll learn to: get focused, overcome self-doubt, set goals, stay on track, bounce back, keep yourself motivated—win job offers! Produced by Bill Frank, high-level career consultant to more than 100 major U.S. corporations. Expert advice by three top human resources executives who've made hundreds of job offers. If your company bought you an expensive outplacement program, this is exactly what you would learn.

Six 30-minute color VHS videotapes
Reg. $349.95
SALE $249.95 (Postage Paid)
10-minute VHS Sneak Preview $14.95

The Job Search Time Manager

A fun-packed 90-day journal and treasury of lists, forms, and worksheets for getting a job offer fast. Besides a daily organizer and "To Do" list, each page is brightened by a high-impact motivational quote, a word of advice from a hiring expert, and a really great cartoon. You'll also find a filing system, secrets of networking and closing the sale, an interview pre-flight checklist and recap form, a weekly progress scorecard, and an expense record. In short, anything and everything you'll need to get organized—and stay organized. Doodle inside, mark it up, make notes in the margins. Play! Have fun! If you're in the job market, you need this book to motivate, excite, and inspire you—and occasionally, to give you a good swift kick!

Paperback, 208 pages
$19.95 (Postage Paid)

Quantity   Please send the following:

_____ **200 Letters For Job Hunters**
8½" x 11" Paperback,
Ten Speed Press $22.95 _____

_____ **Getting FIRED, Getting HIRED:**
Job Hunting From A to Z
Six 30-minute VHS
Reg. $349.95
Sale Price $249.95 _____
10-minute VHS
  "Sneak Preview" $14.95 _____
CareerLab

_____ **The Job Search Time Manager**
8½" x 11" Paperback,
Ten Speed Press $19.95 _____

Colorado residents add
3.7% sales tax   Tax _____
Shipping & Handling   N/C

All prices include shipping & handling
(Priority Mail)   TOTAL _____

Ship To:

Name/Title _____

Firm _____

Street _____

City _____ State _____ Zip _____

Phone _____

Method of Payment (Sorry, No CODs. US currency only):

❏ Corporate purchase order enclosed. P.O. #

❏ Check or money order payable to CareerLab®

❏ Please charge my ❏ Visa ❏ MasterCard

Card Number _____

Expiration Date _____

_____
Authorized Signature

MAIL TO:
9085 E. Mineral Circle, S-330
Englewood, Colorado 80112
(303) 790-0505
(303) 790-0606 FAX
1-800-723-9675

DEAR READER,

<u>WANTED: YOUR ADVICE, IDEAS, AND SUGGESTIONS.</u>

This book is not a one-time event. It is a process, not a product. It is a networking and communications tool, and as such it is never completed. It is always being changed and improved.

If you have job-search materials you think would help others, please send them to me. I'm interested in well-written resumes and job-search letters, especially those that produced interviews or job offers. I also collect job-hunting cartoons and forms or organizers that make the job search easier.

If I use your materials, you'll receive a $25.00 reward and a FREE copy of the next book containing your ideas.

Thank you kindly,

William S. Frank
President
CareerLab®
9085 East Mineral Circle, Suite 330
Englewood, Colorado 80112

$25.00 REWARD

P.S. Be sure to include your name, address, and telephone.